The Kids' Pick-a-Party Book

50 Fun Themes for Happy Birthdays and Other Parties

Penny Warner

Meadowbrook Press
Distributed by Simon & Schuster
New York

Library of Congress Cataloging-in-Publication Data

Warner, Penny.
    The kids pick-a-party book : 50 fun party themes for kids, ages 2 to 16 /
by Penny Warner.
        p.   cm.
    Includes index.
    ISBN 0-671-57966-5 (Simon & Schuster)
    ISBN 0-88166-293-3 (Meadowbrook)
    1. Children's parties. 2. Birthdays. I. Title.
    GV1205.W378   1997
    793.2'1—dc21   97-35061
                                                                              CIP

Editor: Liya Lev Oertel
Copyeditor: Nancy Baldrica
Production Manager: Joe Gagne
Production Assistant: Danielle White
Cover Art: Gwen Connelly
Illustrations: Laurel Aiello

Published by Meadowbrook Press, 5451 Smetana Drive, Minnetonka, MN 55343

BOOK TRADE DISTRIBUTION by Simon & Schuster, a division of Simon and
Schuster, Inc., 1230 Avenue of the Americas, New York, NY 10020

02 01 00 99 98 97   10 9 8 7 6 5 4 3 2 1

Printed in the United States of America

DEDICATION

As always,
to Tom, Matt, and Rebecca

ACKNOWLEDGMENTS

To the students at
Diablo Valley College and Chabot College
who contribute wonderful ideas.

CONTENTS

INTRODUCTION

For many parents, planning a child's birthday party can be overwhelming. There are so many details to consider, you might wonder where to begin. The whole event can seem unwieldy and chaotic when you have to decide

- whom to invite to make the party fun;
- what to set up to create a festive atmosphere;
- what treats to serve that the kids will eat;
- what games to play to get the kids involved;
- what activities to provide to keep the kids entertained;
- what favors to send home with the guests without breaking your budget;
- how to ensure that everything runs smoothly.

The trick to successful party planning is to select a theme. Every birthday or holiday party needs a theme to give it focus. The theme forms the heart of the party and provides the personality, creativity, uniqueness, and detail for the event.

The best way to pick a theme is to ask an expert—your child! Kids know their interests, and those interests can easily become the motif of any celebration. If, however, you and your child need some help choosing a party theme, or if you're looking for something out of the ordinary, check out the suggestions in the following chapters for ideas, directions, and details.

Once you've chosen your theme, simply pick out the invitations, decorations, and party favors to match, and adapt them to fit your needs and the ages of the kids. You'll find that having a central focus for the party helps stimulate ideas and organize your efforts.

Before you select a party theme, consider what type of party you want to host. Below are six distinct party types:

- The Event Party—This party features an event, such as a homemade carnival or ice skating show at the park. You can create the event at home, in the backyard, at the local park, or host the party at an event site, to make it even more authentic.
- The Movie Party—This party is designed around a favorite movie or video: an animated cartoon such as *Aladdin,* a silly comedy such as *Ace Ventura,* or an action-

packed adventure such as *Jurassic Park*. You can take the kids to the theater or show a video right in the party room.

- The Activity Party—This kind of party focuses on a special activity of interest to your child. Swimming, reading science fiction stories, or working with arts and crafts, all make good party themes. Host a swimming party at a pool or beach, have a sci-fi party with costumes and games, or provide arts and crafts materials and let the kids create their own party.
- The Fantasy Party—A fantasy party turns the ordinary into the fantastic. Turn your family room into a forest, your garage into a garden, or your patio into a pirate's den. All you need is a handful of materials, such as crepe paper and cardboard, a giant helping of enthusiasm from family members, and a pinch of imagination to provide the special details that make the fantasy come alive. Voilá! You have a one-of-a-kind celebration in a magical, new world!
- The Special Guest Party—This party has a special guest as its focus. Invite a storyteller who can make a book come to life; a makeup artist to perform miracle makeovers; a musician to teach the kids guitar; a magician to perform feats of magic; a sports figure to talk about the big leagues; a local star to share some behind-the-scenes stories; or simply have someone dress up like a character in keeping with your party theme, such as Batman, Barbie, Power Ranger, or a princess. Let the special guest entertain the kids while you focus on the food, fun, and favors.
- The Outing Party—This type of party involves a special outing. You can visit a variety of exciting sites—from the airport to the zoo. You may want to take the kids to a special restaurant, a kids' theater production, a candy factory, a local campground, a children's museum, a fire station, or an amusement park.

The themes included in *Kids' Pick-a-Party Book* provide suggestions for invitations, costumes, decorations, games, activities, food, and favors. Each party theme also includes a section called Variation that offers additional ideas for that particular theme. And you'll find a few Helpful Hints to help you overcome problems that may arise during the fun. To further personalize your party, use your creativity and imagination to match your child's unique taste and temperament.

From under the sea to outer space—and everywhere in between—*Kids' Pick-a-Party Book* has plenty of party ideas. Now it's time to PARTY!

PARTIES

ABRACADABRA PARTY

To create a magical Abracadabra Party, perform these amazing party-planning tricks that are sure to astound the kids. Then watch what appears right before your very eyes!

INVITATIONS

- Write the party details on white cutouts of a rabbit. Cut out a black hat and make a slit in the hat into which the rabbit "disappears." Leave the rabbit's ears showing, and let the kids pull the rabbits out of the hats to read the invitations.
- Write the party details with a white crayon on white paper to make the invitations appear blank. Include a color crayon with each invitation, and tell the guests to color over the paper to magically reveal the party details!

RABBIT-IN-A-HAT CUPCAKES

1. Bake chocolate cupcakes according to package directions; cool.
2. Set each cupcake on top of an extra-large (about five-inch) round chocolate cookie to form hat and brim. Place on individual plates.
3. Roll vanilla ice-cream balls in coconut.
4. Add M&M eyes and nose to ice-cream balls to make a rabbit face. Stick two triangle wafer cookies on top to make ears. (As you work on each ball, keep the rest frozen.)
5. Set ice-cream balls on top of cupcakes; serve to waiting magicians.

- Buy invisible felt-tip pen sets at a toy store. Write the party details on white sheets of paper with the invisible ink. With each invitation, enclose the pen that makes the invisible writing appear. Tell the guests to color over the invitations to read the surprise information.

COSTUMES

- Ask the kids to come dressed as magicians, complete with capes and hats.

• Hang posters of great magicians, such as David Copperfield and Harry Houdini.
• Cut out classic symbols of magic, such as wands, hats, and rabbits, from construction paper to decorate the walls.

GAMES

• Play Mind Reader. Secretly select and coach a kid ahead of time to be the Mind Reader. When the game begins, "randomly" select this child to be the Mind Reader. Ask the Mind Reader to leave the room, then select a Guilty Person. Have the Mind Reader return to the party. Ask the Mind Reader one question regarding the identity of the Guilty Person. "Magically," the Mind Reader will identify the Guilty Person. Here's the trick: Be sure to phrase the question using the Guilty Person's initials in the first two words. For example, if the Guilty Person is named Bruce Lansky, you might say, "*By looking* around the room, can you tell us who is guilty?"
• Spread out a number of magic tricks on the floor. Have the players close their eyes. Remove a trick. When the players open their eyes, they must guess which trick has disappeared. The player who correctly guesses the missing trick first wins the removed trick and drops out of the game. Continue until all the tricks have mysteriously vanished. (You may want to have enough tricks for all players, so everyone gets something.)

• Provide the kids with magic wands (see Favors) to complete their outfits.

DECORATIONS

• Set up a stage in your party room where the kids can perform their magic acts. Place a sturdy piece of wood on some two-by-fours, or spread a bright sheet or blanket over the floor to serve as the stage. Make a curtain from an old sheet and hang it from floor lamps or tall-back chairs to hide behind-the-scenes preparations.

ACTIVITIES

- Ask the kids to come to the party ready to share a magic trick they've learned. Then stage a magic show and have the kids perform their tricks for the rest of the guests.
- Borrow some books on magic tricks from the library and learn a few simple tricks. Then take each kid aside during the party and teach him or her a trick to perform for the others.
- Try the "Walk through Paper" trick. Give each guest a large sheet of construction paper. Tell the kids you're going to teach them how to step through the middle of the paper. Have them fold the paper in half lengthwise. Then have them cut the paper along each side, as shown. (See illustration.) Tell the kids to open up the paper. Voilá! They'll be able to step through it!

FOLD

cut slits almost to edge, alternating sides

cut along fold, leaving ends intact

open carefully to step through!

VARIATIONS

- Hire a professional magician to perform and teach magic tricks.
- Take the kids to a magic show to enjoy amazing tricks.

HELPFUL HINTS

- Practice a few magic tricks yourself so you know they work well before you try them with the kids.
- Choose tricks that the kids can learn easily.

FOOD

- Make rabbit-shaped sandwiches using a cookie-cutter; fill with the kids' favorite spreads. Have your bakery tint the bread pink for added fun.
- Make Magic Wands. Roll bread-stick dough (available in the grocery refrigerator section) in cinnamon and sugar. Twist two sticks together, and bake according to package direction.
- Serve fortune cookies or Cracker Jacks with surprises inside.

FAVORS

- Send the budding magicians home with a collection of inexpensive magic tricks purchased from a toy or hobby store.
- Give the kids rabbit's feet for good luck.
- Hand out decks of cards so the kids can perform card tricks at home.
- Make magic wands by taping lengths of ribbon to two-foot-long dowels and attaching a silver star cut from poster board to one end. Let the kids decorate their wands with pens, glue, and glitter.

ACTION HEROES PARTY

Superman or Supergirl, Mega Man or Mighty Morphins—whatever your child's favorite superhero, celebrate the favorite character at an Action Heroes Party! Then let the kids power-up, conquer evil, and save the day!

INVITATIONS

- Cut action hero emblems and logos from felt. Cut out the same logos from double-sided iron-on interfacing paper. Iron the two layers together. Mail the logos and the party details to your guests. Tell the guests to ask their parents to iron the logos onto old T-shirts or capes, and to wear them to the party.
- Make a copy of a page from an action hero comic book, white out some of the speech bubbles, fill in the party details, make copies, and mail to guests.

COSTUMES

- Have the kids dress up as action heroes.
- Supply kids with masks, capes, gloves, glasses, or other accessories.

DECORATIONS

- Set the super scene by creating or buying giant cutouts of action heroes and hanging them on the walls.
- Play theme songs from popular action hero shows.
- Make table centerpieces and decorations with small plastic action figures and comic books.

GAMES

- Host an Action Hero Olympics. Prepare a series of challenging feats, varying the games so that everyone has a chance to win. Offer some group games so that large numbers of kids will win, too. Include weight lifting, long jumping, fast running, long-distance ball throwing, balance-beam walking, obstacle course challenges, and relay races.
- Play Super Hearing. Have the kids identify mysterious tape-recorded sounds.
- Play Super Tasting. Blindfold the kids and have them sample and guess foods.

- Play Super Smelling. Blindfold the kids and have them sniff a variety of aromas and name the sources.
- Play Super Vision. Have the kids look at enlarged or reduced pictures of every-day items and guess what they are.

ACTIVITIES

- Make Power Portraits. On construction paper, trace and cut out two body out-lines of each guest. Have the kids deco-rate the outlines—one as front and the other as back—using felt-tip pens, scraps of fabric, puffy paints, and glit-ter. Staple the sheets of paper together, leaving an opening at the top. Stuff the "bodies" with batting or newspaper, then seal the head and prop up the heroes around the party room or table.
- Make your own action hero comic books. Have each guest draw and color a panel featuring his or her favorite action hero character. Assemble the panels to make a funny story.
- Make fabric capes. Have the kids deco-rate the capes with glitter and stars.

ACTION HERO CAKE

1. Bake a sheet cake; cool.
2. Decorate the cake with an emblem from your child's favorite action hero costume, such as Superman, using appropriately colored frosting.
3. Set action figures all over the cake. Give these to the kids after the party.

VARIATIONS

- Take the kids to see an action film or rent a video, such as *Batman, Power Rangers,* or *Ninja Turtles.*
- Have an adult friend come to the party in costume for a surprise visit.

HELPFUL HINT

- Include a list of action heroes on the invitations to stimulate creative choices; some ideas are Wonder Woman, Super Girl, Mighty Mouse, Green Slime, Green Hornet, Spider Man, Flash Gordon, Cat Woman, The Joker, The Riddler, and Atom Ant.

FOOD

- Serve a power party meal, with high-protein drinks, such as Gatorade, and super snacks, such as Power Bars.
- Build a superhero sandwich. Buy two long loaves of sourdough bread and cut off one end of each. Fill the loaves with layers of meat, cheese, tomato, and let-tuce. Place the sliced ends together to create a superlong sandwich!

FAVORS

- Send the action heroes home with small plastic action figures and comic books.
- Hand out the Power Portraits and capes the kids made during Activities.

AROUND THE WORLD PARTY

The kids can go around the world without even leaving home when you gather them for a globe-trotting get-together. Fasten your seat belts!

INVITATIONS

- Write the party information on picturesque postcards showing far-off lands. Or make your own postcards by gluing pictures of favorite vacation spots onto stiff tagboard.
- Create paper airplanes by folding white paper as shown. (See illustration.) Unfold the paper and write the party details inside the fold, using such terms as "arrival and departure times" and "destination." Refold, slip each airplane into a large envelope, and mail.
- Write the party information on the backs of travel posters that depict sites around the world, roll them up, and mail in cardboard tubes. (You should be able to find free travel posters at travel agencies.)

COSTUMES

- Have the kids dress to represent a particular destination. For example: a snowsuit for Alaska, a Hawaiian shirt for a tropical island, a serape for Mexico or South America, clogs and suspenders for the Netherlands, or a sari for India. Assign a place, or let them pick one themselves.

DECORATIONS

- Transform your home into a setting for your world tour with posters of favorite locations (available at travel agencies).
- Decorate the walls with maps. Use one large map as a tablecloth.
- If you have any items from your world travels, set them around the room, or use them to create a table centerpiece.
- Buy foreign books, magazines, and comic books, and place them on the tables for guests to enjoy.

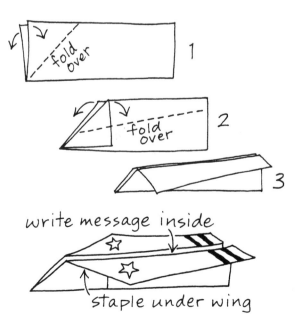

1 — fold over

2 — fold over

3

write message inside

staple under wing

- Display ethnic costumes, and have the kids try them on during the party.
- Play Italian, French, Chinese, African, and other ethnic music.

GAMES

- Play Pack Your Bags. Fill a suitcase with items from different countries, enough for all guests. Divide the kids into two teams, and have them sit in two lines. Open your suitcase, and tell the players you have just returned from a long trip around the world. Give each player an item. To begin the game, the last person in line says the name and the country of origin of his or her item, and then passes the item to the next person in line. That person must then repeat the first item and country, then add his or her own, and pass both to the next person. The team that finishes first wins the game.

WORLD MAP

AROUND THE WORLD CAKE

1. Make your favorite cake mix batter according to package directions.
2. Pour the batter into a large, well-greased, oven-proof bowl. Bake and cool.
3. Carefully loosen the cake from the bowl, and place on a cardboard, doily-covered circle.
4. Make clouds with white frosting, ocean with blue-tinted frosting, and earth with chocolate frosting—to resemble the Earth from a distance.

- Try the Foreign Language game. Find a foreign traveler dictionary with easy-to-say phrases. Choose a simple phrase, such as *"Ou est le McDonalds?"* Have the kids take turns reading the phrases—and acting them out if they need to—while the rest of the guests try to guess the meaning.
- Play Travel Puzzle. Glue two travel posters onto two pieces of stiff tagboard. Cut both posters into large puzzle pieces. Divide the players into teams, and have them race to assemble the puzzles—then name the location.

ACTIVITIES

• Have the kids write to pen pals from other countries. Buy a kids' magazine that lists pen pals. Give each guest stationary and a fancy pen, and have them write to their new foreign friend. Provide comic books and small favors the kids can include with the letters. Drop the letters into the local mailbox.

• Make ethnic costumes. For example, make serapes by providing large squares of loose-weave fabric and letting the kids fringe the ends. Or let them make hats from Germany, Sweden, or Mexico. You

may want to let the kids wrap saris around each other, or have them create their own costumes using yards of colorful fabric. Then have a fashion show.

FOOD

• Ask the guests to bring a potluck dish from another country. Assign each guest a place, or let them choose.

• Make your own international sampler. Offer Chinese appetizers (potstickers), Italian soup (minestrone), Indian salad (curried rice and fruit), Mexican main dish (burrito wraps), French dessert (éclairs), and an English beverage (tea).

FAVORS

• Give the kids poppers filled with little toys from other countries: Fill cardboard tubes with toys, wrap the tubes with crepe paper, and tie both ends with ribbon. (Make a bow only, so it can be easily untied.) Fringe the ends of crepe paper with scissors. Let the kids open the poppers to find the surprises inside.

VARIATION

• Instead of going around the world, make one country the theme of your party.

HELPFUL HINT

• If you don't have a lot of novelties from around the world, borrow some from friends and neighbors.

BAZILLIONS OF BALLOONS PARTY

Have a blast with our Bazillions of Balloons Party. All you need are some inflated ideas, a little "hot air," and a bazillion balloons! Then watch the kids as they try to bat, catch, and pop the party fun.

INVITATIONS

- Create big balloon invitations with party details that grow right before your eyes. Write party details on the surface of an inflated balloon using a permanent felt-tip pen in a contrasting color. Deflate the balloon and watch the words shrink. Place the balloon in an envelope and mail it with instructions to blow up the balloon to read the message.
- Blow up balloons with air or helium and tie off the ends. Write party details on the surface, place balloons in individual boxes, and hand deliver to guests.
- Write party details on a small piece of paper, roll the paper into a tube, and

insert it into a balloon. Blow up and tie off the balloon. Hand deliver to guests. The kids will have to pop the balloon to read the party invitation!

COSTUMES

- Have the kids use balloons to create a unique balloon costume to wear to the party. They might make hats or decorate their shoes with balloons, stuff their

BALLOON CAKE

1. Bake three round cakes in oven-proof bowls; cool.
2. Frost each cake a different color, preferably red, blue, and yellow.
3. Attach a licorice whip "ribbon" to each cake
4. Write a special message on top of each cake "balloon."

the mail box, on the front yard trees, along the roof line, down the driveway, or around the front door to greet your guests as they arrive.

- Fill the party room with balloons—attached to the door handles and along the walls, floating or suspended from the ceiling, for a balloon canopy.

- Cut out balloon shapes from colored construction paper and use them as place mats, wall hangings, and other decorations.

GAMES

- Play Pop-a-Balloon. Tie a balloon around the ankle of each child and let the kids try to pop one another's balloons by stepping on them. The trick is to keep their own balloon from being popped by the other players.

- Write challenges on small pieces of paper for each of the kids, such as "Do a dance," "Kiss a friend," "Sing a song," or "Do a somersault." Stuff one note in each balloon, blow up balloons, and toss them onto the party floor. Have the kids try to pop a balloon. When a balloon pops, everyone must stop moving. The guest who popped the balloon must read the instructions on the note and perform the challenge.

- Play "Who can keep the balloon up in the air the longest" or "Who can pop the most balloons."

clothes with balloons, or wear the balloons around their ankles and wrists. The kids can even use deflated balloons, and glue them to an old vest, apron, or tie. Award a prize—a bouquet of balloons—for best costume.

DECORATIONS

- Decorate with balloons everywhere—the more the merrier. Tie balloons around

ACTIVITIES

- Inflate some long, thin balloons, and teach the kids how to make their own balloon animals. Instructions are available at a library or at party stores.
- Give the kids felt-tip pens, stickers, and other decorations so they can detail their balloon animals. Then add paper cutouts for arms and hands, legs and feet, ears and hair.

VARIATIONS

- Have a clown come to your party and ask him or her to make balloon creatures for all the kids.
- Have a clown come to the party to teach the kids how to make their own balloon animals.
- Plan a water balloon party, get parents' permission, and have the kids bring a set of extra clothes to the party.

HELPFUL HINTS

- Be sure to supervise young children around balloons. Uninflated and popped balloons pose a choking hazard.
- Have lots of extra balloons on hand, so when they pop, the fun doesn't stop!
- Rent a helium tank from a party store to inflate the bazillion balloons easier.

FOOD

- Make lots of round snacks that look like balloons. Serve round crackers filled with cheese spread or peanut butter, carrots or zucchini cut into wheels, Spaghetti-Os served in bowls, or balloon-shaped sandwiches cut with a cookie cutter or a drinking glass.
- Attach "strings" to the balloon treats using thin licorice, string cheese, or other edible "ribbon."

FAVORS

- Give the kids a balloon bouquet to take home. Attach regular balloons onto straws, or tie helium balloons onto long ribbons.
- Send the kids home with a package of variously sized, uninflated balloons.
- Give the kids a pack of uninflated water balloons to enjoy in their own yard.
- Hand out long, thin balloons so the kids can make their own balloon animals at home. Enclose printed instructions for creating a simple balloon animal.

BEARY FUN PICNIC PARTY

For a Beary Fun Picnic Party, all you have to do is invite the bears! But you may want to let the kids come along, too, just for fun!

INVITATIONS

- Cookie bears make great edible invitations. Mix up your favorite gingerbread or sugar cookie recipe. Use a cookie cutter to cut the dough into teddy bear shapes. Bake according to recipe directions. While the cookies are baking, write the party details on Popsicle sticks; you'll need one for each bear. When the cookies are done, remove from heat and immediately insert a Popsicle stick into base of each bear, to form cookie pops; cool. Hand deliver to guests.

COSTUMES

- Have the kids come dressed as bears.
- Tell the kids to use face paints to create their own bear look, or paint their faces at the party as an activity.
- Offer the kids headbands covered with brown fur and decorated with furry ears. Pin a large, brown, pompon tail onto each guest.

DECORATIONS

- If you have a collection of teddy bears, get them out and make them special guests at your party. You can hang them from the ceiling, set them on the furniture, decorate the table with them, or have them peek out from various places in the party room.
- Cut out lots of teddy bears from brown construction paper and place them all over the party room. Name each bear after a party guest, and at activity time, let the kids dress and detail their namesakes.
- Have a giant teddy bear at the front door to greet the guests: Stuff Dad's old clothes with towels and place the "body" on the front porch or on an entryway chair. Set a teddy bear inside the body so its head just sticks out. On the door near the bear, attach a sign that says, "Welcome to a Beary Fun Party!"

GAME

- Play Teddy Bear Tails. Give each kid a "tail" cut from brown felt. Have the kids tuck the tails into the backs of their pants or shirts and sit in a circle on the floor. Choose someone to be the Teddy Bear, looking for his or her tail. Teddy Bear must walk around the outside of the circle, touching each child's back, until suddenly the Teddy Bear grabs one of the kids' tails! As the Teddy Bear runs around the outside of the circle and tries to come back to the open space, the tailless player tries to catch the bear and get his or her tail back. If the tailless player doesn't make it, he or she becomes the next Teddy Bear to look for a tail!

TEDDY BEAR CAKE

1. Bake two round cakes and seven cupcakes; cool.
2. Set one round cake next to the other on a platter to form a bear's head and body.
3. Place two cupcakes at the top for ears, two at the sides for arms, and two at the bottom for legs.
4. Cut the last cupcake in half, leaving the top intact, and set in center of the head cake to make a nose. Let the kids munch on the bottom half.
5. Cover all cakes and cupcakes with chocolate frosting.
6. Make fur with shredded coconut or chocolate sprinkles, add eyes with chocolate chips or tiny Oreo cookies, and make a mouth with red frosting or red licorice.

ACTIVITIES

- Give each kid a large paper teddy bear cut from brown construction paper. Let the kids decorate the bears to look like themselves, using construction paper, fabric, glue, and pens.
- Let the kids make whatever they want using the teddy bear cutouts; some ideas include bear monsters, bear superheroes, or bear cartoon characters. Tape the decorated bears onto the wall until the party is over, then let the kids take their bears home.

ture teddy bears. Then let the kids decorate their bears with raisins, nuts, seeds, coconut, chocolate chips, Rice Krispies, and other goodies. Let them gobble up the bears when finished.

FAVORS

- Give the kids miniature teddy bears. You can find them at craft or toy stores.
- Offer the kids picture books about bears to read at home.
- Hand out bear stickers. They make good and inexpensive favors.
- Send the kids home with little bags of Gummy bears.

VARIATIONS

- Instead of a Teddy Bear Party, have a Baby Doll Party or a Monster Party, and let the kids bring their favorite related toys.
- Have an adult friend rent a bear costume and make a surprise appearance at the party.
- Take a trip to the zoo to see the real bears.

HELPFUL HINTS

- Have everyone bring a teddy bear to the party.
- If some of the kids do not have bears, have a Stuffed Animal Party, and let the kids bring any kind of stuffed toy.

- Make miniature teddy bears using brown socks. Have the kids stuff the socks with newspaper or batting, then tie off the head from the body with a ribbon. Use ribbons to tie off the ears, arms, and legs. Let the kids add details with permanent black felt-tip pens.

FOOD

- Bears like honey, so make some honey dough the kids can play with and eat! Combine half a cup smooth peanut butter with a quarter cup honey and half a cup instant nonfat dry milk. Mix until the mixture reaches dough-like consistency. Divide the dough among the guests, and have them shape the dough into minia-

BIKE AND TRIKE PARTY

For a wild wheelie party, have the kids bring their bikes and trikes to ride for a couple of hours. Then watch the party really start to roll.

INVITATIONS

- Cut out pictures of trikes and bikes from toy catalogs and glue them on the front of folded sheets of construction paper. Draw a path from the bike to the inside of the card. Have the path lead to a picture of your home. Write the party details next to the picture.
- Cut out a picture of a bike and reproduce it on colored paper at a copy store. Cut out the bikes and cut off the wheels. Cut out wheels from different-color paper, and attach to all bikes; use V-clips so the wheels move. Write the party details on the wheels; mail.

BIKE CAKE

1. Bake two round cakes; cool.
2. Set the cakes next to each other on a platter to form bike wheels.
3. Attach a length of rectangular cookies along the top to form a bike frame.
4. Make handle bars out of two peeled bananas.
5. Frost cakes to look like giant wheels with spokes. Use cherries to anchor the spokes in the center of each cake.

COSTUMES

- Have the kids come dressed in biking shoes and brightly colored bike-racing clothes, such as stretch shorts and tops.

DECORATIONS

- Instead of decorating the party room, decorate the bikes, and make that part of activity time. When the kids arrive with their bikes, set the bikes up on the front lawn or backyard patio. Then let

the kids decorate them with crepe paper, streamers, decals, stickers, horns, reflector tape, flags, windmills, and noise-makers. Provide tape, string, and scissors to complete the decorating fun, and have the kids attach the stickers and decals with tape, if you don't want them to be permanent. (You may want to ask the kids' parents regarding permanent decorations.)

- Let the kids decorate their bike helmets, too.

GAMES

- After the kids decorate their bikes, blindfold a selected player. Have the rest of the group mix up the bikes. The blindfolded player must try to guess which bike is his or hers just by feeling—and without wrecking all the decorations!
- Make an obstacle course for the kids to maneuver on their bikes. Award prizes for completion and timing, or award individual points for each stunt along the way.

ACTIVITIES

- When everyone finishes decorating their bike or trike, it's time for a parade. Plan a safe route for your bike brigade, and choose a mature leader to guide the group. Move along the sidewalks and pathways slowly, and head for a destination, such as a park where the kids can ride around freely, or an ice-cream parlor, where the kids can have dessert.
- Award prizes for the decorated bikes, and be sure everyone gets a prize. Have awards for Most Creative, Silliest, Strangest, Scariest, Most Likely to Come Apart, Most Covered with Decorations, and Most Colorful.

FOOD

- If your parade is headed for the park, bring along a picnic lunch to eat while you're there.

VARIATIONS

- Instead of a Bike and Trike Party, have a Wagon Party, a Wheelbarrow Party, a Skateboard Party, or a Hot Wheels Party.

HELPFUL HINTS

- While on parade, be sure there is an adult in the back of the line as well as the front.
- Make sure everyone has a helmet before you begin the bike activities and parade.

- If your parade is going for dessert, be sure to serve some light snacks ahead of time, so the kids won't get tummy aches and lose energy along the way.
- Give the kids trail mix and water bottles to take along on the ride.
- For a perfect bicycle treat, pick up a package of wheel-shaped pasta and boil it according to package directions. Add your favorite cheese and voilá! you have Bicycle Wheel Macaroni and Cheese!

FAVORS

- Give the kids bike accessories to take home; some ideas are horns, reflectors, bike stickers, glow-in-the-dark decals, streamers, bike seat covers, mirrors, decals for bike helmets, or small personalized license plates.

BUGS ARE BEAUTIFUL PARTY

It's time to bug the kids with a Bugs Are Beautiful Party! Kids seem to be strangely attracted to little critters, so why not make that your party theme!

INVITATIONS

- Buy large or small plastic bugs at a novelty or toy store and superglue them to the party invitations or to plain white cards. Write the party details around the bugs and place the cards in envelopes. Drop a few more bugs into the bottoms of the envelopes for an added surprise, and mail to guests.
- Create your own critters from black construction paper. Trace or draw bug shapes on black paper. Cut out the shapes and glue them onto sheets of white paper. Write details (names, origins, favorite foods) about each "party bug" on the white paper, or use metallic paints and write on the bug cutouts. Add party details, and mail to future entomologists.

COSTUMES

- Ask the kids to come dressed as bugs! They can create costumes that replicate their favorite bugs, or make up unique new species.
- Have the kids give their alter egos names, such as Bug Man, Caterpillar Kid, Worm Head, and Scorpion Girl.

DECORATIONS

- Fill the party room with plastic bugs, insects, worms, ants, and other creepy and crawly things. Sprinkle plastic ants on the table, stick Gummy worms in the snack bowl, hang spiders from the ceiling, and spread bugs all over the floor.
- Tuck some insects into a few surprise places to give the kids a little jolt when they reach for a napkin or sit in a chair.

GAMES

- Have a bug race and see how many bugs the kids can spot in the backyard or park in five minutes. Draw sketches of bug types or give the kids bug charts to help them identify the bugs they find.

- Have the kids collect bugs. Give them bug boxes to hold their specimens, and see how many bugs the kids can collect in a set time. Have the kids return the bugs to the yard when the game is over.
- Play Caterpillar. Have all the guests stand in a line, bend over, and hold onto the guest in front of them. Then have the first player in line lead the rest of the "body" in a game of follow the leader. Give each player a chance to be the "head" of the caterpillar and lead the body up, down, and around the yard.

ACTIVITIES

- Make Refrigerator Bug Magnets. Spread out newspaper on the party table. Place bug-making materials on the table, including small pom-poms, felt, wiggly eyes, pipe cleaners, feathers, and other art accessories available at craft or toy stores. Have the kids cut out felt

shapes to use as foundations for their bugs. Then have them glue on pompom bodies and heads, wiggly eyes, and other details. Suggest that the kids make ladybugs, beetles, worms, caterpillars, or create a strange new species. When the bugs are complete, give each guest a strip of magnetic tape (available at craft and hardware stores) cut to fit the length of the felt foundation. Peel off the paper, and stick the magnetic strip to the bottom of the bug. When the bugs are finished, watch them magically stick to the refrigerator!

- Have a Snail Paint. Find snails in the yard and let the kids paint them with nontoxic paints. Have a race with the decorated snails, then return the snails to the yard when they're all tuckered out.

WORMY DIRT CAKE

1. Make a spice or white cake or cupcakes, adding raisins to the cake batter; cool.
2. Frost the cake with chocolate frosting.
3. Sprinkle crushed chocolate wafer cookies on the frosting to look like dirt.
4. Add Gummy worms and other candy bugs to the dirt.
5. Tell the kids to watch for bugs inside the cake, too!

- Make spider webs from cotton candy.
- Create bug nests from coconut or shredded wheat.
- Make fly paper from fruit rolls—then stick candy or plastic bugs onto the fly paper.

FAVORS

- Send the entomologists home with a handful of plastic bugs.
- Give the kids bug boxes to use for studying insects in their yard.
- Hand out books to help identify insects, or give the kids storybooks about bugs, such as *The Very Hungry Caterpillar,* by Eric Carle.

FOOD

- Serve the kids a Lady Bug Salad. Spread lettuce leaves over individual plates. Set a canned pear half in the center of each lettuce-covered plate. Top the pears with red hots candies or pimento pieces to make spots. Set two canned apricot halves on either side of each pear to make wings. Make antennae from strings of celery and top the antennae with cherries or grapes. Make legs using raisins. Serve to hungry insect-eaters.
- Make Buggy Ice Cubes. Place edible candy bugs in the bottom of an ice cube tray, add water, and freeze the tray. When the ice cubes are frozen, place them in party drinks.

VARIATIONS

- Take the kids to an insect museum to study bugs up close.
- Go on a hike and have the kids find bugs along the way. When you locate a new bug, look it up in your guidebook to identify it.
- Have a picnic when you reach your destination, but try not to eat any ants!

HELPFUL HINTS

- Be sure to tell the kids when the bugs are plastic and nonedible and when they can eat the food bugs!
- Don't put plastic bugs inside anything the kids might eat.

CAMP-OUT PARTY

Host an all-nighter in your own backyard campground and watch the happy campers enjoy the great outdoors! Pitch the tent, turn on the flashlights, cook the marshmallows, then hit the sack!

INVITATIONS
- Send the guests a package of freeze-dried food or ice cream that expert campers use (available at sporting goods and nature stores). Write the party details on the outside of the package using permanent felt-tip pen, or tape the invitation to the food packet.
- Send the campers a compass with a sheet of directions to the party, to help them find their way.

COSTUMES
- Have the kids come to the party dressed for camping in the wilderness, wearing hiking boots, camp shirts, shorts or jeans, and hats.

TRAIL MIX CAKE
1. Bake a favorite-flavor sheet cake; cool.
2. Frost with a favorite frosting.
3. Top the cake with trail mix items such as coconut, seeds, chopped nuts, cereal bits, raisins, candies, and chopped dried fruit.

DECORATIONS
- Decorate the tent with streamers, balloons, and funny signs.
- If you don't have a tent, fold a large blanket or tarp over a clothesline, or hang a piece of rope between two trees to make your own pup tent.
- Have a supply of backpacks, sleeping bags, camping gear, comic books, and other camp-related items. (You may

GAMES

- Play Trapped in the Sleeping Bag. Have two kids get inside one sleeping bag, then zip it all the way up the sides, making sure both players have their hands down at their sides. Tell them you hear a bear coming down the path and they have only a few seconds to get out of the sleeping bag, so they'd better move fast! Time the campers to see how long it takes them to get out of the sleeping bag. Then try the game again with another couple of kids, and compare escape times.
- Have a sleeping-bag sack race. Have everyone hop inside their sleeping bags from the start to the finish line.

ACTIVITIES

- Get out the flashlights and take a midnight walk around the neighborhood, under the leadership of an adult.
- Have one group walk around the backyard, leaving clues as they go, such as arrows made from lined-up rocks or a trail of bread crumbs. Then have a second group follow the clues left by the first group.
- Have the kids sit in a circle and share ghost stories.
- Have the kids climb into their sleeping bags and read comic books by the light of flashlights.

want to ask the kids to bring some of their own camping gear to supplement your supply.)

- To add to the atmosphere of a backyard forest, paint glow-in-the-dark eyes on construction paper, cut them out, and staple them around the yard—on bushes, to the fence, on the trees—so it looks like wild animals are keeping an "eye" on the campers in the darkness.
- If you have any tapes of animal sounds, play them when the kids go to bed. Such tapes are available at nature stores.

FOOD

- Roast hot dogs over the open flames of a barbecue or hibachi. After the hot dogs are cooked and tucked into hot dog buns, call them Campers in Sleeping Bags.
- Heat beans in a can and serve as a side dish. (Careful, the can may be hot.)
- Make s'mores for dessert. Have the kids stick marshmallows onto the ends of sticks or straightened coat hangers and hold them over the fire for a few seconds until they are brown (try not to let the marshmallows burn!). Give each kid two

graham crackers and one Hershey chocolate bar square the same size as the crackers. Have the kids make a sandwich, with the crackers for "bread" and the chocolate and melted marshmallow in between. Be sure you have extra ingredients on hand, because the kids are going to want s'more!
- Don't forget trail mix and bottled water or juice for the hike.

VARIATION

- Take the kids to a real campground and have your party in the wilderness! Ask the kids to bring their camping gear, then pitch the tents, and hike around the campground. Be sure to invite a couple of extra parents to help out for safety's sake.

HELPFUL HINTS

- Some kids may be scared of the dark, so have night-lights available outside.
- Consider inviting a couple of parents to join the overnighter, for those kids who need the extra security of mom or dad.
- When walking around at night, have plenty of flashlights, move slowly, and don't go into poorly lit areas.

FAVORS

- Send the campers home with brand-new comic books.
- Give each kid a compass to find his or her way home.
- Give the kids packets of ice cream or other freeze-dried treats to take home.
- Hand out miniature flashlights or other inexpensive camping gear.

CANDY AND CAKE PARTY

Kids love sugar and spice and everything nice, so invite them to a smile-makin' Candy and Cake Party, featuring all their favorite treats.

INVITATIONS

- Buy a bunch of candy bars and carefully remove all the wrappers. Set the candy bars aside. Write the party details inside the wrappers using a permanent felt-tip pen, or insert a separate piece of paper with the party information inside the wrapper. Fold the wrappers back up without the candy, and place them in envelopes to mail to the kids. Save the candy bars for a game.
- If you prefer, send the candy bar, too. Write the party details inside the wrappers, then tape them back together around the candy bars, and mail them in padded envelopes.

COSTUMES

- Have the kids dress up as candies, or use candies as accessories to decorate some sweet-looking costumes. Tell the kids there will be an award for best candy costume, so they should be creative!

DECORATIONS

- Set out colorful candies everywhere in the party room—all sizes, shapes, and kinds.
- Using old cookbooks or magazines, cut out pictures of goodies and make a collage to hang on the wall or to place on the tablecloth.
- Write the kids' names on candy bars and set the candy bars on the table as place markers.
- Spell out the kids' names at each place setting using chocolate kisses.
- Hang suckers from the ceiling.
- Decorate the front door with candy to greet your guests. Glue paper-wrapped candies to large sheets of poster board. Cover the front door with the candy-covered poster board. Watch the delighted faces arrive at your door.
- If you have a Candyland game, use it as a centerpiece.

GAMES

- Have a Candy Bar Taste Test. Unwrap some chocolate candy bars, break them into bits in separate bowls, and let the kids taste each one. Then have them try to guess the candy bar names.
- Unwrap the candy bars and rewrap them in foil. Then let the kids guess the brands just by looking at the shapes.
- Play the Candy Catch Game. Have the kids sit in a circle. Place a bunch of candy bars (one for each player) in the center of the circle. Give each player four playing cards, and place the remainder of the deck in the middle. One player begins by drawing a new card from the deck, and passing it to the player on the left. The next player passes a card to the left and so on to the end, where a card is discarded. Each player tries to collect four of one

suit. When a player has four of one suit, he or she quietly takes a candy bar from the center, while continuing to pass cards. When others notice someone has taken a candy bar, they are to follow suit, grabbing up a candy bar as quickly as possible. The last one to take a candy bar is out, but gets to keep the candy as a consolation prize. Replenish the candy supply, and continue playing until only one player remains.

BOX OF CANDY CAKE

1. Make chocolate and/or vanilla cupcakes; cool.
2. Frost with chocolate frosting.
3. Decorated with tiny candies.
4. Set the cupcakes in a big dress box lined with foil.
5. Close the box lid and cover the entire box with velvet wrapping to look like a giant box of candy, complete with bow.
6. Open the box and serve the giant cupcake bonbons.

ACTIVITIES

- Make LifeSaver necklaces. Have the kids string the candy on yarn or thin shoelace licorice. The kids can then wear the candy necklaces for the rest of the party.

- Make Hamburger Cookies by placing a double chocolate-frosted Oreo cookie between two vanilla wafers. Stick them together using red frosting for ketchup, yellow frosting for mustard, and green frosting for lettuce.

FAVORS

- Send the kids home with a handful of chocolate gold coins.
- Give the kids mysterious candy bars wrapped only in foil so they have to guess what kind of candy it is.
- Offer each guest his or her own personal small box of chocolates.
- Don't forget to send home the LifeSaver necklaces.
- Treat the kids to giant lollipops.

- Have the kids make candy leis by using ribbon to tie together small hard candies wrapped in cellophane.

FOOD

- Serve some nutritious foods that look like candy. Make sandwiches using brown bread and peanut butter and call them Reese's Peanut Butter Sandwiches.
- Make Lunch Lollipops. Layer a slice of bologna, a slice of cheese, and a slice of bread; roll the layers into a tube; and slice into ¼-inch-thick rounds. Stick a pretzel or a toothpick into the side of the round to keep it together and to make a lollipop.

VARIATIONS

- Take the kids to a candy factory to see how candy is made.
- Make your own candies using plastic candy forms available from a bakery store. Fill with caramels, nuts, and marshmallows.

HELPFUL HINTS

- To make sure the kids don't overeat on the sweet stuff, offer them candy bags to store the goodies for later.
- Make regular "candy snack" times when each kid is allowed to eat one treat. Signal snack times with a bell or whistle.

CARNIVAL/CIRCUS PARTY

The circus is coming to town and it's bringing a party with it! Turn your house, yard, or garage into a big top celebration, with lots of goodies, games, and kooky clowns. It's carnival time for kids of all ages!

INVITATIONS

- Make clown masks using construction paper, felt-tip pens, sequins, and glitter. Use a glue gun or super glue to attach a red rubber ball for a nose, then cut out eye holes. Tie a string to either side of each mask, write the party details on the inside of masks, and mail them in large envelopes.

BURIED CLOWN CAKE

1. Bake a sheet cake; cool.
2. Frost the cake with chocolate icing.
3. Make Clown Cones: Scoop round balls of ice cream into sugar cones; turn the cones upside down onto a plate or cookie sheet; and decorate the ice cream clown faces with frosting tubes, using the cone as the clown's hat. Keep in freezer until cake time.
4. When ready to assemble, place Clown Cones on top of the cake, ice cream side down, evenly spaced, one for each child, so the clowns look as though they are buried beneath the cake and only their heads are sticking up.

- Insert invitations into boxes of circus animal crackers. Place each box of crackers into another small box to keep the crackers from being crushed in the mail.

COSTUMES

- Ask your guests to come dressed as clowns! Suggest they dress in colorful, baggy thrift-shop clothes. Decorate their faces with face paint.
- Have the kids dress like circus animals or as one of the side show characters.
- Award costume prizes for funniest, most creative, scariest, saddest, and so on.

DECORATIONS

- Make your own big-top tents by hanging sheets and blankets or crepe paper streamers from the ceiling.
- Create carnival game booths using large cardboard appliance boxes painted with poster paint.
- Fill the party room with multicolored balloons for a festive atmosphere.
- Place stuffed animals and clown dolls around the party room for an added attraction.
- Distribute items used in a circus, such as hoops, nets, batons, and so on, throughout the party room.

GAMES

- Have the party "animals" do some circus stunts, taking turns being the ringmaster who gives orders. The kids can jump through hoops, leap over ropes, duck under sticks, and step through tires and other obstacles while behaving like animals.
- Play carnival games using the cardboard-box booths. Include such games as Ring the Soda Bottle with rings cut from tagboard; Gone Fishin' with sticks, string, and magnets for fishing poles; Penny Platter with pennies tossed on a plate; Catch a Goldfish with real goldfish in a kiddy pool that the kids try to catch with their hands; and Water Gun Shooting Gallery with squirt guns to shoot small plastic bottles off a ledge.

ACTIVITIES

- Have each kid draw a clown face on a large sheet of paper using felt-tip pens, crayons, or paint. See who can come up with the funniest face.
- If the kids don't come with their faces already painted, have them use face paint to decorate each other's faces to look like clowns.
- Instead of having the kids wear costumes to the party, provide a variety of funny, old, thrift-store clothes at the party, and have them mix and match to create their own crazy clown look.

VARIATIONS

- Go to the circus or the carnival if it's in town and enjoy a real big top and Ferris wheel. (Be sure to have enough adult supervision.)
- Find out when your local communities are hosting festivals, and make one of those events the focus of your party.

HELPFUL HINTS

- Be sure to have lots of prizes on hand for the games—for both winners and losers—so everyone has a good time and feels successful!
- Have the kids win tickets instead of toys at the carnival booths, then have them cash in the tickets for a prize at the end of the party.

FOOD

- Set out plates of animal crackers for snacking.
- Make Animalwiches by cutting animal shapes out of bread with cookie cutters. Fill with favorite spreads.
- Cut out slices of bread, cheese, and meat using animal cookie cutters. Place all animal shapes on a platter and let the kids assemble their animal sandwiches as they would a puzzle.

FAVORS

- Send the kids home with small stuffed animals you'd find at a circus.
- Make popcorn balls and give them to the kids to take home.
- Let the kids keep the small toys they win at the game booths.

COOKS IN THE KITCHEN PARTY

What's the recipe for a really great party? Take a handful of invitations, add some decorations, throw in some games and activities, and add a heaping measure of do-it-yourself food. Mix well with a roomful of guests and enjoy your Cooks in the Kitchen Party!

INVITATIONS

- Buy or make blank recipe cards for your guests. Write down the recipe for a special treat on one side, and the party details on the other side (phrase the party details to read like a recipe). Then send the recipe card, along with the special treat (the one for which you wrote the recipe), to your guests.
- Send small cooking utensils along with the invitations, and ask your guests to bring them back to the party.

COSTUMES

- Ask the kids to come dressed as chefs, or provide large white men's shirts for your guests. You can find inexpensive shirts at thrift stores.
- Make big fluffy chef's hats out of white or colored crepe paper. First make a headband from the crepe paper. Cut out a big circle from crepe paper and puff it out in the middle. Wrap the headband around the outside bottom of the pouf, and staple or glue the pouf and the band together. Place the hats on the chef's heads as they arrive.

DECORATIONS

- Decorate the party room to look like a special restaurant. Include menus, a fancy tablecloth, your best silverware, and other special touches.
- Decorate the kitchen with lots of cooking supplies tied with ribbons.
- Put up pictures of food, set out a variety of cookbooks, and group ingredients together for a game to be played later.

GAMES

- Set collections of ingredients together, one collection for several teams of two to three kids. For example, you may have pizza ingredients on the counter, cookie ingredients near the stove, and omelet supplies by the sink. Have the kids move from station to station, and try to guess what the ingredients will make.
- Play the Food-Tasting Game. Blindfold the kids; serve them a food you have cooked before the party, and have them guess what the food is. Then reveal the treat.
- Play Name That Ingredient. Have the kids taste a new food and guess the ingredients. Put something unusual in your recipe to make guessing a challenge, such as a banana in peanut butter cookies.

EASY-BAKE MINI CAKES

1. Buy a large muffin tin or a set of small round cake pans.
2. Bake large muffins or small cakes, one for each guest; cool.
3. Give each guest a cake or muffin.
4. Set out bowls of variously colored frostings, frosting tubes, candy sprinkles, and sugar decorations. Give the kids plastic knives.
5. Let the kids frost and decorate their individual cakes.

ACTIVITIES

- Divide the kids into small groups, and have each group create a new food with ingredients you provided. For example, you may give one group the ingredients for chocolate chip cookies, but add several optional ingredients, such as seeds, dried fruit, coconut, and so on, so the kids can be creative.
- After the groups create their food masterpieces, let them name their treats. Then have a taste test to determine which creation tastes yummiest, strangest, most creative, and so on.

FOOD

- Eat what you cook! Make mini-pizzas from English muffins, macaroni and cheese with unusual noodles, do-it-yourself tacos, peanut butter chocolate chip

cookies, two-flavor ice-cream pie, kitchen-sink trail mix, confetti pasta salad with colorful cut-up vegetables, or salt-water taffy.

FAVORS

- Send the kids home with recipes of the foods you've made at the party, so they can cook the same foods at home.
- Give your guests kids' cookbooks, such as *Kids' Party Cookbook* or *Kids Are Cookin'*. (See the order form in the back.)
- Offer the kids a special food treat.
- Give the kids their own special cooking utensil, such as a turkey baster filled with candy, a ladle filled with nuts, or an egg whip filled with cotton candy.

VARIATIONS

- Take the kids to a cooking school and let them see the experts at work.
- Ask a local restaurant for a behind-the-scenes look at the kitchen, then stay for lunch or dinner.

HELPFUL HINTS

- Check with parents to see if any kids have food allergies. Make sure to avoid those foods.
- Have the kids wear aprons—cooking can get messy.
- Keep the recipes quick and easy, and make recipe cards enlarged and illustrated, so they are easy to follow.

CRAFTY ARTISTS PARTY

Let the kids create their own party, with a Crafty Artists Party! All you need are art supplies—paints, crayons, paper, and glue—to give your gathering a creative start in art. Everything, from the invitations to the favors, is sure to be a masterpiece!

INVITATIONS
• Send your guests Magic Rainbow invitations. Completely cover white postcards with different colors of crayons. Paint over the crayon with black poster paint. When the paint is dry, scratch off the party details using an opened paper clip. Watch the colorful words appear under the black paint.

ARTIST'S PALATE CAKE
1. Bake enough cupcakes for all the guests; cool.
2. Tint white frosting with food coloring to create a variety of colors. Cover each cupcake with a different color frosting.
3. Cut out an artist's palate from poster board. Arrange the cupcakes in a three-quarter circle on top of the palate and place in the center of the table.
4. Lay a few paintbrushes nearby for effect.
5. Or bake a rectangular cake and let the kids "paint" the cake with small paint brushes and bowls of tinted frosting.

• Send the kids small pack of crayons. Write the party details in crayon inside the boxes.

COSTUMES
• Ask your guests to dress like artists and wear smocks.
• Provide old shirts for the kids to wear at the party. Inexpensive shirts are available at thrift ships. Make the smocks look more authentic by adding little color splashes using acrylic paints, felt-tip pens, or puffy paints.
• Give each child a beret to wear with his or her outfit.
• Attach strings to paintbrushes, and have the kids wear the paintbrush necklaces

• Cover the table with a white sheet of paper, and let the kids decorate their own tablecloth with the art supplies.
• Hang up prints of famous artists to inspire the kids' creativity.

GAMES

• Play Pass the Portrait. Give each child a sheet of white paper lined into eight horizontal sections. Have each kid draw a face on the top section, then fold back the section with the head and pass it to the next player. Tell them to draw a neck and shoulders, without looking at the head. Fold back the next section, hiding the shoulders, and continue passing the papers until the entire body has been drawn, piece by piece. Unfold the portraits to see the funny results! Have the guests name the portraits and hang them on the walls. (If you prefer, pass around one sheet at a time.)

around their necks. (Make sure to carefully supervise young guests. Necklaces can pose a strangulation risk to small children.)

DECORATIONS

• Set up easels, craft areas, and art supplies, including paints, crayons, felt-tip pens, clay, wood, stencils, glitter, sequins, ribbon, glue, tape, stapler, scissors, and string.
• Cut out construction paper frames and stack them along walls. Use the frames to frame the kids' artwork during the party.

ACTIVITIES

• Have the kids use art materials to create works of art.
• Frame and display the finished products. Give everyone an award for creativity.
• Finger-paint with vanilla pudding tinted with food color, so the kids can taste-test their work as they create a picture.
• Show the kids how to decorate T-shirts with puffy paints and permanent felt-tip pens.

- Make Baker's Clay by combining four cups flour, one cup salt, and one and one-half cups water. Let the kids make whatever they want, then bake the dough in the oven at 250 degrees for one hour, or until firm. Paint the clay creations when they're cool.

FOOD

- Serve painted sandwiches by letting the kids "paint" on white bread slices with food coloring. Then toast the bread to make it firm.
- Have the kids design their own crafty snacks from peanut butter playdough by mixing one cup smooth peanut butter with half a cup honey, and one cup non-fat dry milk. Let the kids play with the dough for a while, then let them eat it

when they are finished. (Make sure that everyone washes their hands before playing with the dough, so they don't eat any glue or glitter!)

VARIATIONS

- Take the kids to an art class or studio and watch the artists create their work.
- Ask the instructor to include the kids in an art or craft activity.
- Visit an art museum that features art that appeals to kids.

HELPFUL HINT

- Crafty Artists parties are messy—but that's half the fun. Be sure to cover the party area with newspapers and drop cloths so you won't have to worry about the mess.

FAVORS

- Send the kids home with watercolor paint sets, crayons, or colorful felt-tip pens.
- Give the kids any other art supplies, so they can continue the creative process at home.
- Give the kids how-to-draw or coloring books.

CREATIVE CAREERS PARTY

Take a look into the future to see what the kids will be when they grow up. Give them a chance to come as anyone they want to be—teachers, doctors, astronauts, dog catchers, rock stars, police officers, even presidents! It's time to get a job!

INVITATIONS

- Mail the kids job application forms you've designed yourself, using a real application as a model. Substitute party questions here and there, such as "Are you available to party from 2:00 P.M. to 4:00 P.M. on Friday?"
- Send the guests a copy of the want ads from the newspaper, adding your own "party want ad" in the middle of the listing. Have it read something like this: "Wanted: party attendee, willing to eat large quantities of cake and ice cream, play silly games, and have tons of fun. Send RSVP, résumé ASAP."

COSTUMES

- Have the kids come dressed in outfits that represent their favorite occupations.
- Tell the kids to come dressed as what they want to be when they grow up.
- Suggest that the kids find items at a thrift store to create their costumes or make them out of crepe paper.
- Send each kid a hat and have the kid create a costume to go with it.

DECORATIONS

- Decorate the party room with items that represent different careers. Hang a stethoscope from the ceiling to represent a doctor, place a briefcase on the table for a lawyer, tack alphabet posters to the wall for a teacher, and put up pictures of rock stars for the future singers.

Job Application
Name: Sean
Address: 33 Oak St.
  Centerville
Job: Teacher
Duties: Can you party at 3:00 pm on Saturday?

Happy Birthday! S.T.

I Love my job!

PAYCHECK
Naomi
for one ice cream cone

• Display a collection of hats from various careers. You may have a fire hat, police hat, sailor hat, detective hat, baseball hat, construction hard-hat, and army helmet. You can find hats at thrift stores, costume stores, and party stores.

GAME

• Collect a variety of clothes and accessories that represent a number of occupations, and place the items in individual bags or suitcases. Choose some obscure careers as well as some obvious ones to make the game interesting. Have one player choose a bag and try on one article of clothing, then have the other players try to guess what he or she is supposed to be. If the kids can't guess, have the player add

BRIEFCASE CAKE

1. Bake a rectangular cake; cool.
2. Frost the cake with chocolate frosting.
3. Cut fruit roll-ups into a handle shape to create a handle.
4. Add the birthday child's initials (or the initials of the guest of honor) in yellow frosting as a monogram (and add Happy Birthday for a birthday cake).
5. Try other designs, such as a blackboard for a teacher, a space ship for an astronaut, or a star-shaped cake for a rock star.

another article or accessory until someone finally guesses the correct occupation. Some ideas for career outfits include pizza maker, pool cleaner, dog groomer, fashion model, electrician, window cleaner, dance instructor, grave digger, bank teller, and garbage collector.

ACTIVITY

• Before the party begins, collect several large appliance boxes. Cut off the tops and bottoms of the boxes, cut along one side, then open the boxes into four panels. Be sure there is one panel for

FOOD

- Eat foods that are traditional for each career. Serve donuts for police officers, apples for teachers, hero sandwiches for construction workers, pizza for pizza makers, and so on.
- Set up a buffet table so the kids can pick and choose.

FAVORS

- Send each guest home with a book about jobs.
- Give each kid a key chain to start a collection of keys.
- Hand out address or appointment books.
- Give each kid one of the hats used for decorations.
- Give the kids phony paychecks that double as gift certificates at the local ice cream parlor.

each guest. Draw a basic outline of a person on each panel. Cut out the face area with an X-Acto knife. Have each guest paint a panel, giving the body clothes, shoes, hair, and other details. Offer pictures to use as suggestions. You may have pictures of police officers, superheroes, cartoon characters, and so on. When the bodies are finished, have each child stand behind his or her panel and place his or her face into the head hole, while the other kids enjoy the new look. Take lots of pictures!

VARIATION

- Instead of staying home for the party, take the kids out to explore new career opportunities. Visit the zoo to find out what it's like to be an animal trainer, a factory to see how things are made, or a fire station to see the firefighters on the job.

HELPFUL HINT

- When you send out invitations, send the kids ideas for career choices to stimulate their creative juices.

DEEJAY DANCE PARTY

Hey, kids! It's All-Dance Radio bringing you the latest in rap, hip-hop, rock and roll, punk, new-wave, country, and soul! You choose the music style and the party will keep the beat!

INVITATIONS

- Write the party details on sheet music (made to looks like song lyrics), add a few notes, and mail your party song to guests.
- Make your own invitation cassette tape by having a deejay announce the party information, or impersonate a deejay yourself. Set the party talk against a background of dance music. Then mail the cassette tapes to all your guests.
- Select a time period or style of music, and play only hits from that era or style, such as sixties music or hip-hop songs.

MUSICAL CAKE

1. To make the cake look like a giant CD or album, bake the batter in a round pan.
2. Frost the cake with white frosting for a CD and chocolate frosting for an album.
3. Write song titles and names of groups on top of the cake using frosting tubes, or make up new groups using the guest-of-honor's name.

COSTUMES

- Have the kids dress in dance costumes from different musical eras.
- Have the kids dress for a sock hop, a hippie love-in, or a country-western line dance.
- Have the kids wear fancy socks to the party for dancing, and make them remove their shoes when they arrive.

DECORATIONS
- Cut out music notes from black construction paper and hang them on the walls and from the ceiling.
- Cover the walls and doors with album and CD covers and posters of favorite rock singers and groups.
- Rent a jukebox, if you can afford it, and ask the supplier to fill it with your favorite hits.
- Hire a professional or amateur deejay to keep the music coming.

GAMES
- Play Name That Tune. Prepare a cassette tape of songs taped from the radio or from your music collection. Play the songs a few seconds at a time as you tape-record them, then record a few seconds of silence between each music segment, so guests have time to write down or call out their answers. Offer a variety of songs, from hip-hop and pop to country and soul.

- Have a Copy Me Dance. Select one person as the leader. Every time the leader changes to a new dance style, everyone must follow along until someone else is tagged to take over the lead.

ACTIVITIES

- Have a dance contest and award prizes for a number of categories, such as the wildest, goofiest, fastest, or most entertaining.
- Offer radio station giveaways. Every so often, stop the music, call out a music trivia question, and have the audience guess the answer. Whoever answers first gets a musical prize, such as a cassette single or a picture of a rock star.

VARIATIONS

- Rent a local dance club for the party, and take the kids out dancing.
- Hire a professional or teenager to give the kids dance lessons for the latest steps.
- Take your guests to a rock concert that's appropriate for the kids' ages.

HELPFUL HINTS

- Provide a variety of music, rather than just one kind, so everyone will enjoy the party.
- Clear off an area in the house or garage for dancing, and provide chairs and benches for resting between dances.

FOOD

- Make small or large pizzas to look like CDs or albums, and write the names of favorite groups on them using bits of pepperoni, bell pepper, or mushrooms.
- Serve food associated with various musical eras, such as burgers and malts from the fifties, brownies and fruit juices from the sixties, and so on.

FAVORS

- Send the rockers home with cassette or CD singles.
- Give the kids posters of rock stars.
- Be creative and give out other music-related items, such as harmonicas, music note paper, or books about favorite rock stars.

DINNER AND DRAMA PARTY

Treat the kids to a formal affair with a Dinner and Drama Party. Pick out a play, musical, or show that the kids will want to see, then offer a before- or after-dinner party to complete the festivities!

INVITATIONS

- Send formal invitations—engraved, computer-generated, or hand-written using gold ink on white paper or silver ink on black cardstock paper. As part of the party information, explain that the party will include dinner and a show. Mail the cards in double envelopes to make them look even more impressive.
- Include some homemade theater tickets or photocopies of original tickets inside the envelope.
- Create a fancy dinner menu, and include the party details alongside the food choices. Mail menus in large envelopes.

COSTUMES

- Ask the kids to dress in formal attire—suits, party dresses, and so on.
- Have the kids dress in black and white only, and make the party a black-and-white formal affair.
- When the kids arrive, pin real or artificial corsages or boutonnieres on their outfits, offer imitation tiaras or top hats, or provide inexpensive white cotton

gloves. These items are usually available at thrift or photography stores.

DECORATIONS

- Since part of the party will take place at the theater, fix up the party room to look like a theater lobby, with theater posters of *Cats, Grease, Guys and Dolls,* and other popular shows decorating the walls.

- Dress up the room by tacking up holiday lights along the ceiling.
- Play show tunes for background music.
- If you're hosting the dinner party at home instead of going out, block off the dining area with sheets or blankets to give the room a feeling of intimacy. Then set the table with your best tablecloth and dishes, and have adult friends serve as waiters.

GAMES

- Play word games at the table during your pre- or post-theater dinner. Write down phrases from popular shows or movies and have the kids guess the play or film titles.
- Hand out descriptions of special scenes from favorite shows and have the kids act out the scenes for the rest to guess.

FANCY PETIT FOURS

1. Buy petit fours at the bakery or make your own mini cakes by cutting a sheet cake into squares and freezing them for easy handling.
2. Cover the kids with aprons or smocks to protect their fancy clothes.
3. Let the kids decorate their own petit fours using frosting tubes and decorations.
4. Before serving, place the decorated mini cakes in the center of the table for an eye-catching centerpiece!

- Play segments of popular songs from movies or shows and have the kids guess the titles.
- Prepare dinner foods that were featured in movies or shows, and have the kids guess their sources. (See Food.)

ACTIVITIES

- Have the kids make their own tiaras, using plastic headbands as foundations. Let them use a glue gun to attach stiff tagboard in gold or silver around the rim. Let the kids decorate the tiaras with sequins, glitter, beads, and other baubles.

- Choose dinner selections made popular in movies and have the kids guess the movie source for each dish. For example, serve soup from *Oliver,* pizza from *Ninja Turtles*, bread from *Les Miserables*, meat pies from *Sweeney Todd*, chocolate bars from *Willie Wonka,* and Reese's Pieces from *E.T.*

FAVORS

- Send each kid home with a tape of the play or movie soundtrack.
- Give the kids movie coupons and tins of popcorn.
- Hand out playbills, posters of movie stars, T-shirts related to the play, or books on which the movie or play was based.

- Provide the kids with plain, inexpensive sunglasses, and let them create fancy, Hollywood-style glasses using glitter, rhinestones, and puffy paints.
- Buy a large poster of a movie or Broadway star, cut out the figure and face, and glue it to a large piece of cardboard. Pose each kid next to the star and take Polaroid pictures.

FOOD

- Serve a fancy, seven-course meal in your dining room restaurant: start with soup and salad and end with hot chocolate and dessert.

VARIATIONS

- Instead of hosting dinner at home, take the kids to a fancy restaurant.
- If you plan to have the dinner at home, you may want to show a movie video at home, too, and pretend you're all going to the theater! (This would also be easier on the budget than going out to a movie or play.)

HELPFUL HINTS

- This party can get expensive, so keep the number of kids to a minimum.
- Choose matinees or lunches for your dinner and drama experience.

GHOSTS AND GOBLINS PARTY

Give the kids a chill thrill with a Ghosts and Goblins Party! Host the haunting on Halloween—or give a good scare any time of the year! Turn the garage into a haunted house or the backyard into a scary cemetery, and make the party frightening, festive, and fun!

INVITATIONS

- Make masks from stiff tagboard, cut to fit a child's face. Decorate the masks with puffy paints, sequins, feathers, and stickers to turn them into whatever you like—Frankenstein, Wolfman, Jason, or Freddy, for example. Write the party details on the backs of masks. Attach an elastic string through holes on either side of each mask. Send the masks to guests for an inviting scare. Have the kids wear their masks to the party.
- For added fun, fill the invitation envelopes with a few plastic bugs, ants, or gummy worms.
- If you prefer, send the kids blank masks and ask them to decorate them and wear them to the party.

GRAVEYARD CAKE

1. Bake a chocolate sheet cake; cool.
2. Top with softened chocolate ice cream.
3. Crush chocolate wafer cookies to look like finely ground dirt, and sprinkle over ice cream.
4. Stick Gummy worms into the cake, half in and half out.
5. Stick oval cookies into the cake to make gravestones. Write funny names on the "graves" with frosting tubes.
6. Refreeze before serving so the ice cream doesn't melt.

COSTUMES

- Ask the kids to come dressed as a favorite monster, creepy creature, or bad guy.
- Award prizes for all kinds of costume categories, such as scariest, funniest, hardest to make, hardest to wear, most creative, most authentic, most disgusting, and so on.
- When the kids arrive, provide them with sheets of colored crepe paper, tape, string, and a stapler, and let them design their own costumes.

- Create a Pet Cemetery where mangy wild animals look for food. Have someone dress as a dog, a bear, or other animal, and give them large soup bones to hold. Have them make wild growling noises and threatening gestures as kids pass by.
- Make a Witches Caldron. Dress the witches in long, gray wigs and black dresses, color their fingernails black, black out a tooth or two, and have them stir a caldron with a broom. Inside the caldron, place wet noodles, Jell-O, or water with dry ice.
- Set up a Monster-Making Machine. (See Activities.)

DECORATIONS

- Create a haunted house in the garage or party room. Cover the windows with black paper and set up scary stations. Have the kids weave through the haunted house one at a time.
- Set up a Mad Scientist Laboratory. Have someone dress as a Frankenstein monster and lie on a table among bubbling concoctions (use dry ice and colored water in clear bowls). Add plastic tubing and kitchen utensils, such as tongs, basters, and a garlic press, to serve as bizarre scientific instruments.
- Make a Dead Body Storehouse. Dress friends as accident victims, with torn clothes, and fake blood and scars. Have them lie on the floor and come to life from time to time, by sitting up, grabbing a passing foot, or screaming.

GAME

- Play Body Parts. Have the kids sit in a circle in dimly lit room while you make up a story about a mean, old witch who falls apart, piece by piece. As you talk about each body part, pass around a paper bag lined with a plastic bag, and have the kids feel inside without looking. The bag should contain the "body part" that fell off, such as peeled grapes for eyeballs, a canned apricot for a tongue, popcorn kernels for teeth, cooked spaghetti for brains, a large peeled tomato for a heart, cooked macaroni noodles for intestines, a slab of Jell-O for the liver, and so on. Have the kids guess what you used for the body parts, then reveal the foods.

ACTIVITIES

- Create your own monsters using cardboard boxes or old clothing. Divide the kids into teams of three or four players. Give each team a variety of arts and crafts materials, along with boxes and clothes, and have them create Frankenstein monsters using their imaginations. Display the monsters at the end of activity time and award prizes to each team.
- Make a Creepy Crawly Critter Collection. Place a bag of plastic or candy bugs and worms into a large bowl, mix with Jell-O and wet noodles, and have the kids dig through in the bowl to find the critters.
- Turn the kids into monsters. Create a tunnel out of large cardboard boxes, making windows along the way. Have the kids climb through the tunnel, and as they come to a window, apply fake blood and scars, masks, and so on. The kids come out of the tunnel looking like monsters!

VARIATIONS

- Take the kids to a local haunted house and let them enjoy a real scare.
- Take the kids to a scary movie playing at a local theater.
- Rent a scary video. When the kids are watching quietly, jump out and say "Boo!" to give them a real fright. Watch the popcorn fly!

HELPFUL HINT

- If any kids are really scared, let them in on all your secrets so they know it's all in fun.

FOOD

- Eat the "body parts" similar to those you passed around (use only fresh items that haven't been handled!).
- Serve the kids' favorite foods, but give the snacks gruesome names, such as Swamp Pudding, Eyeball Fruit Salad, Spaghetti Brains and Meatballs, Green Gooey Gopher Gut Yogurt, or Anthill Ice Cream with Chocolate Ant Sprinkles.

FAVORS

- Send the kids home with Gummy worms or other edible critters, or give them plastic bugs and rubber snakes.
- Give the kids monster makeup kits, wax lips and teeth, and masks.
- Give the kids scary books about monsters.
- Offer cassettes of creepy music.

HAWAIIAN LUAU PARTY

Take the kids to the tropics with a Hawaiian Luau Party—right in your own backyard! Slap on the suntan lotion and grab the grass skirts—it's time for some fun in the sun!

INVITATIONS
- Use vacation postcards featuring a South Pacific beach. Write, "Wish You Were Here!" on the photo side of the postcard—then print the party details on the back. Mail to your guests.
- Create your own airline tickets, good for a free trip to your tropical paradise. Write the party details on the ticket to read as destination, time of departure and arrival, and other party information.
- Create a brochure, writing the party information as an advertisement for a tropical paradise.

COSTUMES
- Ask the guests to come as hula dancers, King Kamehameha, bathing beauties, or even tacky tourists, complete with loud Hawaiian print shirts, straw hats, sunglasses, and cameras.
- When your guests arrive, dress them up with grass skirts made from sheets of crepe paper.
- Ask your guests to bring bathing suits to the party.

DECORATIONS
- Turn your yard into a tropical paradise with crepe paper streamers, torches or holiday lights, and big pictures of colorful fish and marine life.
- Hang up posters of tropical islands.
- Decorate the table with postcards of various beaches.
- Make a sandbox and fill it with sand toys.
- Fill a kiddy pool with water for a splash in the "ocean."
- Cut out palm trees from large sheets of construction paper and tack them to the fence.

GAMES
- Find Pirate's Treasure. Bury some toys in the sand and let the kids dig them out. When they find a toy, they get to keep it, but they must drop out of the digging and allow other players to find the treasures.

- Play Musical Pools. Set large pans of water in a circle, enough for all but one player. Play a ukulele as the kids, in bathing suits, march around the pools of water. When you stop playing the music, the kids must scramble for a pool and sit down. The player who does not find a pool is out of the game. Remove one pan of water and continue playing until only one player remains.
- Have a Limbo Contest and see how low they can go. Hold a broomstick or bamboo stick four feet above the ground and have the players try to duck under it by bending backwards. Play some music as the line limbos under the limbo stick. After everyone has had a turn going under the stick, lower it half a foot and go again. Keep playing until only one player remains. The remaining player gets a prize.
- Get out a Hula-Hoop and have a contest to see how long each player can keep

the hoop in the air. Try this game while wearing grass skirts. Younger kids may have some trouble keeping the hoop in the air for any length of time, so have them jump through the hoops instead.

HAWAIIAN ISLAND CAKE

1. Bake a rectangular cake; cool.
2. Cover half the cake with white frosting tinted blue, to look like the sea.
3. Cover the other half of the cake with white frosting and sprinkle brown sugar on top to look like sand.
4. Set toy Hawaiian dancers on the sand and have a tiny shark coming up out of the ocean.
5. Use candles as tiki torches.

ACTIVITIES

- Give the kids coconuts and let them make funny faces out of the coconuts. Point out the two dark circles that form the coconut "eyes," then give the kids puffy paints, regular paints, or felt-tip pens to create crazy coconut heads. When they're finished, hammer a large nail into the top of each coconut, insert a straw into each hole, and let the kids drink the coconut milk.

- Make a watermelon basket by cutting a watermelon in half lengthwise, using a zigzag cut. Open the watermelon halves and scoop out the insides to make two bowls. Fill the bowls with a variety of fruit, including the scooped out watermelon.
- Make pineapple boats by slicing a pineapple in half lengthwise, removing the pineapple inside, and refilling with pineapple chunks, cherries, raisins, and coconut.
- Serve Kid Kabobs by skewering cubes of ham, cheese, pineapple, and cherries on wooden skewers. Let them wash it all down with Hawaiian Punch!

FAVORS

- Send the kids home from their Hawaiian vacation with sand toys, sunglasses, and beach towels.
- Give the kids grass skirts and Hula-Hoops.
- Let the kids wear their candy leis home.

- Make LifeSaver candy leis by letting the kids string together LifeSaver candies to form necklaces. Or have the kids make leis out of cellophane-wrapped candies by tying them together with a ribbon.
- Teach the hula and put on a show!

FOOD

- Have a Hawaiian luau with lots of tropical food, such as fruit salad, fruit kebabs, bananas dipped in marshmallow and coconut, kiwi slices, pineapple wedges on toothpicks with cherries on top, watermelon balls served in a carved watermelon shell, scooped-out oranges filled with sherbet, and so on.

VARIATIONS

- Have your Hawaiian Luau at the beach!
- Invite real hula dancers to entertain the kids.

HELPFUL HINT

- If you have water at the party, be sure to watch over small kids and nonswimmers.

ICE- AND ROLLER- SKATING PARTY

Skaters rule the party scene! Strap on the skates and head for the rinks for a rolling good time. Or set up your own rink at the park, playground, or on the sidewalk and skate away!

INVITATIONS

- Get a picture of the local rink and make photocopies for all the guests. Write the party details on the backs of the pictures and mail to the kids.
- Buy some long shoestrings—the kind found on skates—and write the party details down the sides; mail.
- Send skater decals along with party invitations.

COSTUMES

- Have the kids come dressed as Olympic skaters with fancy outfits for the ice or roller rink.

SKATING RINK CAKE

1. Bake a sheet cake; cool.
2. Frost the cake with white frosting to make ice.
3. Add little, plastic skating figures, available from cake decorating shops or a bakery.
4. Write the name of the guest of honor in cursive; attach a skater at the end of the name, to make it look as though the skater just etched the message.

- Make matching T-shirts for your skating crowd, so you can keep track of your group at the rink. Create a name for your skating club and use that name to decorate the T-shirts.
- Have the kids decorate their own T-shirts with puffy paints and glitter.
- Have the kids come to the party dressed as punk skaters.

DECORATIONS

- You won't have to worry about decorations if you go to a rink—the place is ready to go. But if you rent a private room for the party, bring along balloons, crepe paper, and other decorations, and spiff up the place while the kids are skating.
- If you're at the park, playground, or on the front sidewalk, add a few decorations to give your location a party atmosphere. For example, decorate the pavement with some sidewalk chalk, which will wash away with a hose or the next rain.

GAMES

- Ask at the ice or roller rinks about games and activities they provide.
- If you are at a park or playground, play Musical Skates. Make a large circle using cardboard stars, using enough stars for all but one skater. Have the kids skate around the stars while a portable cassette player plays music. When the music stops, the kids must race for a star. The player who doesn't find an empty star is out. Remove a star and play again. Repeat until only one player remains.
- Try Follow the Leader. Have one player skate around the area any way he or she likes, while the others follow. When two minutes are up, blow a whistle and have the leader touch another player. That skater becomes the new leader, and he or she then leads the group in a creative skate.
- Play Skate for Money. Stand on the edge of the rink or playground with a handful of play money. As the skaters circle the rink, on each round they must, without

stopping, try to grab a "dollar" from your extended hand. Set a time limit on the game, and when the game is over, have the kids count how many dollars they made. Then let them spend the money on small prizes.

ACTIVITIES

- Bring along a cassette of skating and dance activities and play them at the park or playground. For younger kids, try "Hokey Pokey," "London Bridge," and "Ring around the Rosy." For older kids, try a country line dance or a square dance.
- Teach the kids one special skating trick, such as "shoot the duck" (squatting down on one foot with the other leg extended), skating backwards, skating in pairs, or skating connected in a long line.

VARIATIONS

- Take the kids for a day of skiing.
- Have a teenager teach the kids to skateboard.
- Play a game of ice hockey!

HELPFUL HINTS

- If the kids have differing levels of skating ability, have extra helpers on hand to give support, instruction, or guidance.
- Don't forget the knee and elbow pads!

FOOD

- Skating burns up energy and calories, so have plenty of good food on hand.
- Have a barbecue at the park. Hot dogs are great—tasty and portable.
- Make a variety of sandwiches to keep the snacks easy for those on-the-go skaters.
- Provide plenty of liquids throughout the party. Store refreshments in plastic bottles that the kids can carry with them.

FAVORS

- Give the kids a free pass to the local skating rink so they can have another day of fun.
- Hand out Polaroid pictures of the kids skating, as a surprise memento.
- Give the kids skater decals and bumper stickers.

INQUIRING SNOOP PARTY

What's the scoop? An Inquiring Snoop Party! Let the guests read all about it in a special edition invitation! Then give the mild-mannered reporters a peek into the fast-paced newspaper world!

INVITATIONS

- Create a mock-up invitation using a real newspaper front page. First, type the party details, formatted to look like a special news column. Cut and paste your column between a couple of real newspaper stories. Then photocopy the entire page, making enough for all your guests. Mail the invitations or, if possible, insert your paper into your guests' morning newspapers.
- Create your own personal newsletter using desktop publishing software; add pictures, headlines, and other details.

COSTUMES

- Have the kids come dressed as newspaper people—reporters, photographers, gossip columnists, movie reviewers, obituary writers, even managing editors.
- Suggest that the kids find their costumes at a local thrift shop, where they're sure to have trench coats, hats, and other newspaper-related accessories.

DECORATIONS

- Hang newspapers on the walls to create the feeling of a news room. Spread newspapers over the table as a tablecloth.
- Make paper hats from newspapers for the kids to wear.
- Create phony headlines about the guests and post them around the room.
- Search the libraries for copies of newspapers from the guests' birthdays, and use them as place mats. Give them as favors to take home.

GAMES

- Play Headlines. At the library, search through newspapers or news magazines and write down events that happened over the past year. Form questions using the information you've accumulated, and have the kids guess in what month each event took place.
- Play Headlines with news photos instead of headlines.
- Instead of having the kids guess the month, make the game easier by having them place the events in order.
- Have a Word Search. Give each player a sheet of newspaper. Call out a word. Whoever finds that word first on the paper wins a prize.
- Play the Comic Strip Game. Cut out one color comic strip for each guest from the Sunday paper. Cut the strips into individual squares and place them in envelopes. Distribute the envelopes to

guests and see if they can put the strips together in the correct order. Once everyone finishes, exchange the envelopes and play again.

- Vary the Comic Strip Game. Mix all the squares together and have the kids try to pick out the comic strips that go together—in the correct order!

DAILY NEWS CAKE

1. Bake a sheet cake; cool.
2. Frost the cake with white frosting.
3. For a birthday cake, write a Happy Birthday headline across the top.
4. Draw columns on the cake using chocolate frosting and a fine-point tube.
5. Fill the columns with horizontal lines to simulate type.
6. Add smaller headlines to complete the page.

ACTIVITIES

- Have the kids create their own newspaper using construction paper, felt-tip pens, and photographs cut out from magazines.
- Fold newspapers into hats or boats, using instructions from library books that feature paper folding.

cones using Crisco tinted with food coloring. Set them on the table for the kids to admire. If the kids try to sneak a taste, they're in for a big surprise. (Warn the kids if the food is not edible.)

- Have the kids cut up headlines and combine them to make silly new headlines. For example, the headlines "Dead Skunk Found in Park" and "Cold Weather Expected Today" could become "Dead Skunk Expected Today."
- Let the kids draw their own comic strips.

FOOD
- Pick out a recipe from the food section of the paper and make it for the party. Display the food page on the wall or at the table while the kids enjoy the treat.
- For fun, make up some fake foods that look good enough to eat, but aren't—the kind food stylists use for the newspaper. For example, make beautiful ice-cream

FAVORS
- Send the kids home with copies of the newspaper front pages from the days they were born. Obtain newspapers from library files.
- Give each kid a book featuring a popular newspaper comic strip, such as Calvin and Hobbes or Garfield.

VARIATION
- Arrange to visit a newspaper office and get a tour of the place. Let the kids see real reporters, photographers, printers, and editors at work.

HELPFUL HINT
- Newspaper ink rubs off easily on the hands, so keep some wet wipes nearby to clean up the mess.

IT'S A MYSTERY PARTY

You never know what's going to happen when you host a mystery party because—it's a mystery! Play detective, set the clues, and keep the guests guessing with lots of surprises, puzzles, and crimes to solve.

INVITATIONS

- Send puzzling invitations for the kids to solve. For example, write the invitations in your own creative code. The next day send the key to the code; that way the guests will have to wonder for a little while what the invitations say before they can read them!
- Give the kids clues to find the party invitations. Don't tell them what they're looking for, only that it's hidden somewhere on their property.

MYSTERY CAKE

1. Bake a sheet cake; cool.
2. Slice the cake into individual pieces, one piece for each guest. Be sure to keep the slices together.
3. Scoop out a tiny amount of cake from each slice.
4. Fill the holes with small toys, and carefully turn the cake over.
5. Cover the cake with frosting. Decorate it with question marks made with frosting tubes.
6. Serve the precut slices, and warn the kids there's a surprise inside each slice!

- Write the party invitations, cut them into puzzle pieces, and mail the pieces in envelopes to your guests.
- Mail the pieces of the invitation puzzles one at a time, instead of all at once!

COSTUMES

- Have the guests dress as favorite detectives, crime solvers, police officers, or spies.
- When the kids arrive, give them disguises, such as wigs, hats, glasses,

moles, and so on. Then have them create new identities to go with their costumes.

DECORATIONS

- Make the party room dark, spooky, and mysterious. Decorate the walls with masks, costume pieces, and cobwebs; cover the walls and windows with black paper; and dim the lights.
- Set up a cave by draping blankets and sheets over the furniture. Then have the party "underground."

GAMES

- Have a Mystery Crime Hunt. Divide the kids into teams, and have a scavenger hunt for mysterious items you've set out ahead of time in the party room or the yard. When the kids collect all the items, have them figure out what crime goes with the "evidence." For example, for a jewelry heist, have the kids find a necklace, a mask, fingerprints, a screwdriver, a getaway bag, and a false mustache.
- Play Decipher. Divide players into teams, give each team paper and a pencil, and tell them to design codes for the other team. Have them solve the codes.
- Play Touch-and-Tell. Wrap a number of small items. Have the kids sit in a circle. Pass the items from player to player, and have them guess the item. The player who guesses correctly keeps the item and drops out of the game.

ACTIVITIES

- Have the kids make code books using Morse code, Braille, sign language, or other methods of communication. Then have the kids relay messages back and forth, singly or in teams.
- Before the party begins, tape-record noises from everyday life. During the party, play back the tape, and have the kids guess the mystery sounds.
- Get a book on fingerprinting, and teach the kids how to lift fingerprints.

FOOD

- Serve Mystery Soup. Have each guest bring a can of soup with the label removed. Combine all the soups in a large pot, heat, and serve.
- Blindfold the kids before serving snacks; then have them guess what they are eating.
- Have a surprise Popcorn Explosion. Spread out a sheet and have the kids sit around the edges. Place a popcorn

maker in the center and prepare popcorn according to package directions—but DO NOT cover the popcorn maker. Let the kids watch the popcorn pop onto the sheet. Make sure everyone stays away from the popper while it's on so they don't get sprayed with hot oil or kernels. Let the kids gobble up the popcorn when the popping is done.

VARIATIONS

- Visit a police station or jail and see what goes on behind the scenes.
- Ask a police officer or detective visit the party to talk about police work.

HELPFUL HINT

- Don't make the puzzles too difficult, or they won't be fun to solve. Keep them simple and give lots of clues!

FAVORS

- Hand out mystery puzzles and One-Minute Mystery books to enjoy at home.
- Give the kids Mystery Candy. Unwrap candy bars and cover them with foil—for the kids to guess what the candy is.

KARAOKE PARTY

Grab the microphone and gather the guests for a sing-along Karaoke Party! Kids love to perform their favorite songs, so let them become the next Madonna, Elvis, or Barney for a few musical hours!

INVITATIONS

- Sing your invitation! Buy some inexpensive blank cassettes. Write your lyrics—the party invitation—then sing them into a microphone accompanied by background music. Copy the tape for your guests and mail in padded envelopes.
- If you can't carry a tune, write the party details on blank sheets of music paper and mail to guests.

COSTUMES

- Have the kids dress as their favorite pop or rock singers so they're ready for the stage!
- Suggest a musical style, such as a fifties or sixties singer, a lounge or grunge singer, or a country or kiddy singer.

DECORATIONS

- Decorate the party room with posters of favorite musical artists.
- Get out your CDs, cassette tapes, and records, and spread them around the room for inspiration.
- Cut out music notes from black or colored construction paper and hang them from the ceiling and on the walls.

- Cover the table with a white sheet of paper, draw score lines to make it look like giant sheet music, then add music notes.
- Write lyrics from favorite songs on sheets of white paper and use them as place mats.
- Set up a stage so your young performers can sing their stuff. To complete the look, add lighting, a curtain, and chairs for the audience.

GAMES

- Play Name That Tune. Have the kids in the audience guess the song performed by each singer.
- Play another game of Name That Tune by turning the radio dial and guessing the singers and songs.
- Play karaoke tunes without the lyrics and try to guess the songs.
- Play You're Next! Have the kids sit in a circle. Start the karaoke music and choose one player to begin. Hand him or her the lyrics to the song, and have him or her sing for a minute or so. Then suddenly pass the words to another (unsuspecting) player who must take over the song. Continue until the song is over and everyone has had a turn.

ACTIVITIES

- Divide the guests into teams and have them create their own lyrics to popular songs. Then have the teams perform the new songs to one another.
- Teach the kids a song in sign language and have them perform it as a group.

SHEET MUSIC CAKE

1. Bake a sheet cake; cool.
2. Frost the cake with white frosting.
3. Make score lines using chocolate frosting tubes.
4. Create music notes with chocolate chips.

VARIATION

- Go to a karaoke restaurant that allows children, and let the kids put on their own show. Call ahead to arrange the time and songs.

HELPFUL HINTS

- Write song lyrics in large print for young kids.
- Choose songs that are popular with kids today.
- Let the kids do songs together if they are shy about performing alone.

- Videotape the kids' performances so they can watch themselves when they're finished singing.

FOOD

- Serve foods from favorite songs, such as spaghetti from "On Top of Spaghetti" or candy treats from "The Candy Man."
- Make a display of music notes using stick pretzels and raisins, then let the kids help themselves to the decorative, tasty "music."

FAVORS

- Give the kids song tapes and sheets of song lyrics, so they can sing their own tunes at home.
- Hand out copies of the karaoke tapes made at the party.

KOOKY COOKIE PARTY

Everyone loves cookies, so why not have a party that offers cookies from start to finish?! Invite the cookie monsters to the party, open the cookie jar, and watch the kooky fun begin!

INVITATIONS
• Bake one-of-a-kind cookie pop invitations that will delight your guests. Mix a favorite recipe of hearty cookies—sugar, gingerbread, or peanut butter works best. Cut dough into large circles or cookie cutter shapes and bake according to directions. Remove from oven and insert Popsicle sticks into warm cookies to make cookie pops. Cool, then decorate with frosting tubes, adding the party details on the cookie and the Popsicle stick. Tie a ribbon around the stick, place the cookie pops in small boxes with tissue paper, and hand deliver to guests.

COSTUMES
• Have the kids be creative and dress as favorite cookies.
• Have the kids use cookies to decorate hats to wear to the party.
• Make cookie costumes when the guests arrive. Use large sheets of poster board, construction paper, and felt-tip pens. Cut out large circles, rectangles, or other shapes from the poster board, depending on the shape of the cookie you want to create, such as Oreo cookies, wafer cookies, or Animal Crackers. Cover the poster board with construction paper, or color with felt-tip pens. Make two matching shapes for each guest, and attach them at the shoulders with string or ribbon.

DECORATIONS
• Cut out pictures of cookies from magazines or old cookbooks and glue them onto construction paper. Use the posters to decorate the party room. Hang cookie cutouts from the ceiling or tape them to the walls of the party room.
• Decorate the tablecloth with drawings, cutouts, or real cookies.

- Use cookie cutters tied with ribbons as decorations.
- Set out cookie cookbooks for added decoration.
- Make a giant cookie to greet the guests at the door. Cut out a large circle from brown poster board and decorate it with real cookies.

GAMES

- Have a Cookie Contest! Buy a variety of cookies and break them into small bites, so there is one piece of each type of cookie for each guest. Place each broken up variety into a separate paper bag. Pass the bags around one at a time, and have the kids take a taste without looking. Have the kids write

down their guesses, and see who can name the most cookies.
- Try a Cookie-Bite-Off. Have one player taste a piece of cookie. If that player can identify the cookie type, he or she goes on to taste the next cookie. If the player cannot name the cookie, that player drops out of line and the next player continues. Play until only one player remains.

OREO COOKIE CAKE

1. Bake two round chocolate cakes; cool.
2. Frost the sides of one layer with chocolate frosting.
3. Decorate the sides with chocolate sprinkles.
4. Cover the top of the frosted layer with white frosting, marshmallow cream, or vanilla ice cream, about one-half inch thick.
5. Place the second round chocolate cake on top of the first layer.
6. Frost the top layer with chocolate frosting and decorate with chocolate sprinkles.

ACTIVITIES

- Have the kids invent their own new cookie, using ingredients from popular cookie recipes, such as peanut butter, chocolate chips, sprinkles, nuts, and so on. Divide the kids into groups and have a taste test at the end of the cookie creation to see which recipe tastes best.
- Have the cooks shape the cookies into large monster faces, decorated with

bake about five to ten minutes longer than the recipe requires. Check often to see when it is lightly browned. Remove the giant cookie from the oven, cool, and transfer it to a piece of cardboard cut to size. Decorate with frosting tubes, just as you would a cake. Let the kids break off chunks at serving time.

• Serve your treats with Milk-and-Cookie Shakes. Combine one cup milk, one cup vanilla ice cream or frozen yogurt, and two to three Oreo cookies in the blender for each guest. Pour into glasses and serve immediately.

frosting and sprinkles. Whoever has the funniest, scariest, or strangest monster cookie wins a prize.

• Host a cookie exchange. Ask the kids to bring two to three dozen favorite home-made cookies. Place the cookie collections on the table, count them to figure out how many cookies each kid can take, and let the kids take that number of cookies from each pile to take home.

FOOD

• Shape favorite sandwiches with cookie cutters, so the sandwiches look like cookies!

• Have a bakery tint a loaf of bread pink or blue for added fun.

• Make a giant cookie instead of a cake by mixing up a cookie recipe and spreading the entire cookie batter onto a well-greased cookie sheet. Shape the cookie into a circle or a heart, then

FAVORS

• Send the kids home with a box of store-bought cookies, a bag of homemade cookies, or a collection of cookies from your cookie exchange.

• Give each guest a cookie book and some cookie cutters.

VARIATIONS

• Take the kids to a cookie factory to see how cookies are made.

• Have a baker come to the party to make cookies.

HELPFUL HINTS

• Offer lots of food alternatives so the kids don't get overloaded on sweets.

• Use cookie cutters to give alternate foods interesting shapes.

LIONS, TIGERS, AND BEARS PARTY

Time to monkey around at a Lions, Tigers, and Bears Party. Turn your party room into a real zoo! Invite the wild animals over for some animal-antics, and see if you can tame them before feeding time!

INVITATIONS

- Welcome your guests to your homemade zoo with homemade Cage Invitations. Using a yearbook or borrowed snapshots, photocopy pictures of the invited guests. Cut out cards from black construction paper and fold them at the side. On the outside of the card, cut out bars to make a cage. Place the picture of one of your guests on the inside of the card, so he or she appears to be inside the cage when the card is closed. Write the party details in white ink on the inside of the card.

ZOO CAKE

1. Bake a rectangular cake; cool.
2. Frost the cake with chocolate frosting.
3. Sprinkle the cake with brown sugar to look like dirt.
4. Set small plastic animals on the cake.
5. Let each kid have an animal to take home!

COSTUMES

- Have the kids come dressed as favorite zoo animals.
- Dress the kids up as animals when they arrive. Use large sheets of crepe paper to create the costumes.
- Have the kids create costumes for one another using crepe paper.
- Instead of costumes, make or buy animal masks or snouts for the kids to wear.

DECORATIONS

- Make the party room look like a zoo, with cages cut from large cardboard appliance boxes. Paint the boxes with poster paints, cut out the fronts to look like cages, and cut back openings for the "animals" to enter. Label each cage with an animal type and wait for the creatures to come to the party.
- Decorate the party room with stuffed animals (have the kids bring stuffed animals to the party).
- Be sure to have a camera ready!

GAMES

- Play Animal Noises. Write the names of animals or draw pictures of animals on individual cards. Some examples include lions, tigers, bears, and so on. Pass the cards out to the kids as they sit in a circle. Have them make the sound representing the animal on their card. Have the other group members try to guess the animal.
- Play a variation of Animal Noises. This time, act out the animal's walk, instead of imitating the animal's sound.
- Play Pull My Tail. Stick cloth or paper animal tails onto the backs of each player with tape. Have the kids try to collect as many tails as they can from one another, while trying to keep their own tails. Whoever collects the most tails wins a prize.

ACTIVITIES

- Let the kids use face paints to create animals on each other's faces. Have some animal books handy to give the kids ideas.
- Have a professional face painter come to paint the kids' faces.
- Make necktie snakes. Have each kid bring a necktie, or provide neckties by shopping at a thrift store. Open the large end of the ties by pulling out the threads, then stuff the tie with polyester fiberfill, using rulers or sticks to push the stuffing deep into the ties. When the ties are stuffed, glue them closed using a glue-gun or sew them up. Glue on buttons or pom-poms for eyes or use puffy paints. Then glue or sew on red felt tongues.

VARIATIONS

- Go to the local zoo and have a real zoo party!
- If you know someone with an exotic pet, such as a boa constrictor, an alligator, or a parrot, have them bring it to the party.

HELPFUL HINT

- This party is better outdoors, where the "wild animals" can run free, so set your cages outside if possible.

FOOD

- Serve the kids zoo food, such as peanuts, popcorn, hot dogs, and sodas.
- Cut sandwiches into animal shapes with cookie cutters.
- Let the kids make individual animal pizza faces using English muffins as the heads. Offer condiments to use as decorations, then bake in the oven until hot and ready to eat.

FAVORS

- Give the kids plastic animals to enjoy at home.
- Let the kids keep their animal masks.
- Hand out books about animals.
- Give each kid a small stuffed animal.
- Find recorded songs about animals and give them to the kids.
- Hand out posters featuring funny animals.

LOCOMOTION PARTY

Since kids are always on the go, why not provide them with a way to get there—a Locomotion Party! Hop on board and take a trip to party land. You never know where you'll end up!

INVITATIONS
- Create giant tickets inviting your guests to the Locomotion Party. Copy a plane or train ticket, or make up your own using construction paper and felt-tip pens or a computer and printer. Make the destination the party house and include arrival and departure times.
- Send the kids postcards with "Wish you were here!" written on the front and the party details written on the back.
- Tuck the invitations inside travel brochures, or format them to read and look like travel brochures.

COSTUMES
- Ask the kids to come dressed as transportation workers, such as railroad engineers, flight attendants, cruise ship directors, or bus drivers.
- Have the kids come dressed as tourists ready to travel the world.

DECORATIONS
- Hang up posters of faraway lands and exotic locations.
- Play music from foreign countries in the background.

- Cut maps into pieces to use as place mats. Use a couple of unfolded maps as a tablecloth.
- Set the scene by creating the interior of a plane, train, or boat. For a plane, set up two rows of chairs, use a TV as the in-flight move screen, and serve food on TV trays. Drape a sheet from the ceiling in an arch to form the plane's roof. Do the same for a train, except for the movie screen. For a boat, set up lawn chairs in a row, serve the food buffet-

style, and draw a shuffleboard game on the patio. Hang fishnets on the walls. Make portholes using construction paper, with fish on the other side of the "glass," and hang them on the walls.

GAMES

- Play Where in the World? Cut out sections of a map and have the kids try to guess where in the world they belong.
- Give clues about famous sites around the world and have the kids guess the location.
- Show postcards or posters from foreign lands and let the kids identify the places.
- Play Musical Airplane Seats (or train or bus). Set up enough chairs for all but one guest. Play music and have the kids walk around the chairs. When you stop the music, the kids scramble for a chair. Whoever does not find a seat is out. Remove one chair and play again. Continue playing until only one player remains.

- Have the kids act out a mode of transportation, such as riding in a carriage, skating, skiing, or riding in a spaceship. Let the other players guess what they are riding.

ACTIVITIES

- Provide cardboard boxes about the size of a microwave oven, so the kids can fit them around their bodies. Have one box for each guest. Decide whether you want to make train cars, automobiles, individual planes, or something else in

TRAIN CAKE

1. Bake or buy one small loaf cake for each guest.
2. Have the kids decorate their loaf cakes to look like train cars, using a variety of frostings, decorations, and candies.
3. When finished, line the cakes up to make a train.

• Serve packaged nuts before mealtime, like they do on airplanes.
• Have adults walk up and down the aisles like flight attendants, waiting on the kids while they enjoy their in-flight meals.

FAVORS

• Give the kids key rings to take home. Attach their initials or a toy plane, train, or car.
• Hand out address books so the kids can keep in touch.
• Provide small picture books with a travel theme.
• Give the kids compasses to help them find their way home.

which the kids can travel. Then cut windows, doors, and holes for arms and legs as needed. Let the kids paint the boxes to look like train cars, automobiles, and so on. Then have the kids travel around outdoors in their new transporters.

FOOD

• Serve individually wrapped "airline" food on TV trays while the kids sit in their seats.

VARIATIONS

• Take the party on the road to visit an airport, cruise ship, train, or fire station. If you call ahead, you can often arrange a behind-the-scenes tour for the kids.
• Go to a car show or race.
• Take the kids to a small-car driving range for fun.

HELPFUL HINT

• If offering a wide variety of transportation themes seems too much, keep the party simple by focusing on just one type of locomotion.

MAKEOVER PARTY

Invite the kids over for a whole new look with your Makeover Party! Include makeup, hair styles, clothes, and accessories. Then get out the camera and shoot the new models on the runway!

INVITATIONS

- Get photos of the kids from parents or yearbooks; photocopy each picture twice. Make cards from construction paper. Glue one picture on the outside of the card and one on the inside. Write "Before..." as a heading for the outside picture, and add warts, bad hair, freckles, and all sorts of funny face additions. Write "After..." on the inside picture, with the party details on the facing page. Then add fancy makeup and

NEW YOU CAKE

1. Bake a round or rectangular cake; cool.
2. Find a hand mirror that's smaller than the cake, wash it, and place it on top.
3. Frost the cake all around the mirror and down the sides.
4. Add candles around the mirror and light them to create a "lighted mirror."
5. Let the kids look into the cake and see their own reflections, then blow out the candles, remove the mirror, and eat the cake!

hair to the inside picture using felt-tip pens, to create a "makeover."

COSTUMES

- Have the kids come dressed in casual clothes, but ask them to bring along fancy outfits to change into when the makeover is complete.
- Ask the kids to bring what makeup they have, or provide some yourself.

- Mount smaller pictures on construction paper and use them as place mats.
- Display all the makeup and hair-care products you'll be using for the makeovers.

GAMES

- Play Beauty Shop. Cut out products from beauty magazines, omitting the names of the products (or blacken the names out with a felt-tip pen). Glue the pictures onto construction paper, with the names of the products written lightly on the backs. Have the kids sit in a circle. Hold up one picture at a time and have the kids write down the names of the products (tell them to keep the answers secret). When all the pictures have been displayed, read the answers out loud to see who guessed the most correct answers.
- Play Beauty Shop using TV jingles. Record jingles on a cassette tape, leaving out the names of the products. Play the tape for the kids and have them guess the products.

DECORATIONS

- Set out some portable mirrors around the room so the kids can see the makeovers take place.
- Get out cameras—video and Polaroid— to take photos and to use them as props.
- Hang up pictures of famous models and draw mustaches, glasses, and warts on their face. Write "Before" across the top.

ACTIVITIES

- Do makeovers on one another, using makeup, hair products, and accessories. Use a beauty book as a guide and have each guest pick out a picture to follow. Buy inexpensive makeup kits for each of the guests, have the guests bring their own makeup, or get cosmetic samples from makeup counters. Discourage the guests from sharing makeup to reduce the risk of infections.
- Have the kids try exotic new looks for fun.
- Provide lots of variety in makeup, such as blush, lipstick, powder, eyeliner, mascara, and so on.
- Have the kids try on false eyelashes, fake moles, false fingernails, and so on.
- Let the kids do one another's hair.
- Dress the kids up in their fancy clothes, let them model their new look, and take glamour pictures.

VARIATIONS

- Take the kids to a beauty college, and have the students practice their skills on your guests.
- Have a beautician come to the party to teach the kids how to do their own makeovers.

HELPFUL HINT

- Keep wet wipes and paper towels handy for continuous cleanup. Makeup can get messy!

FOOD

- Serve elegant foods, such as canapés (tiny sandwiches) and bubbling apple juice (apple juice mixed with club soda or ginger ale). Serve the food on your best dishes and use champagne glasses for beverages.
- Make fun-to-eat finger foods so the kids don't have to stop to eat. Let them snack as they work on one another.

FAVORS

- Send the kids home with new hair brushes, makeup, barrettes, fake fingernails, small mirrors, ribbons, or anything else you used during the Makeover Party!

MUSIC MAKER PARTY

There's music in the air when you host a Music Maker Party—and you don't even have to carry a tune! Provide the young musicians with musical opportunities and watch the party turn up the volume!

INVITATIONS

- Set your invitation to music. Use a portable cassette player to record a tune from your own one-kid band. Sing the party details as lyrics, and mail cassettes in padded envelopes.
- Write party details on sheet music and mail to guests.
- If you have a friend who likes to sing, hire him or her to deliver "Singing Invitations" right to your guests' doorsteps!

COSTUMES

- Have the kids come dressed as musical instruments (tell them to use their imaginations).
- Ask the kids to come dressed as favorite musicians—grunge singers, lounge lizards, pop stars, or conductors!

DECORATIONS

- Cut out music notes from black construction paper and hang them from the ceiling or tape them to the walls.
- Use musical instruments as table centerpieces, and use sheet music as place mats.

- Play a variety of music in the background when you're not performing your own musical entertainment.

GAMES

- Play Musical Chairs in a whole new way! Set up chairs in a circle, enough for all but one of the guests. Give each child a kazoo or inexpensive toy horn. Begin the game by playing the kazoo as all the guests walk around the chairs. Stop playing whenever you want. When the playing stops, all players must scramble

for a chair. The player who does not find a seat gets to play the kazoo for the others. Continue until only one player remains.

- Play Instrument Identification. Have musicians play their instruments one at a time for your cassette recorder, or tape-record a variety of instruments from your own music collection. Pause between tunes, and let the kids try to guess what instrument was played.
- Play the Instrument Identification game using the music from Peter and the Wolf.

ACTIVITIES

- Make your own instruments. Get a book from the library on making simple musical instruments for kids. Make an oatmeal drum, a pie-pan tambourine, an elastic bracelet with bells sewn on, two-pot-lid cymbals, sandpaper wood blocks, toilet-paper kazoos, rice-and-bottle maracas, and so on. When the instruments are finished, line the kids up for a con-

cert, or march them around the block for a musical parade. Be sure to videotape the concert for playback later.

- Put on fingerplays set to music when you finish making your instruments. Have the kids decorate their fingertips with felt-tip pens to make small people or animal. Then tell the kids to make their "puppets" dance to the music.

FOOD

- Serve food that makes noise! To create a musical meal, try crunchy celery and carrot sticks, cheese and cracker sandwiches, apple-walnut fruit salad, sodas or milk shakes with straws, and lots of

DRUM CAKE

1. Bake two round cakes; cool.
2. Frost one layer with chocolate frosting, place another layer on top, and cover with chocolate frosting.
3. Decorate the sides with tube frosting, making crisscross designs to look like the sides of the drum.
4. Top the drum cake with small kazoos, harmonicas, or lots of silver bells.

popcorn. Then take turns "playing" the food to make a meal band!

FAVORS
- Let the kids take home the musical instruments they make.
- Give the kids songbooks or fingerplay books so they can learn new tunes at home.
- Hand out inexpensive harmonicas, kazoos, noisemakers, whistles, or other music-makers.
- Buy small music-box inserts at a fabric or hobby store and drop them into the kids' pockets. Then press their pockets and listen to the surprise music!

VARIATIONS
- Take the kids to a concert. Try rock, country, or even classical music that appeals to kids, and let them enjoy the world of music.
- Have a guitar player come to the party to teach the kids how to play a few chords.

HELPFUL HINT
- If you have valuable musical instruments at the party, be sure to teach the kids how to handle and respect them, or keep the instruments off limits to avoid damage.

OLYMPICS PARTY

Let the young athletes flex their muscles for a gold medal at your Olympics Party. Set up the various events, put the challengers through the hoops, and watch them all come up winners!

INVITATIONS

- Invite the kids to your Olympics Party by awarding them their first gold medal! Cut out cardboard circles and cover them with gold foil or spray-paint them with gold paint. Attach a colorful ribbon so the kids can wear their medals around their necks. Write the party details in permanent felt-tip pen on one side of the medal. Write "Winner" on the other side. Mail to the athletes.

GOLD MEDAL CAKE

1. Bake two round layer cakes; cool.
2. Tint white frosting with yellow food coloring.
3. Frost one layer with the yellow frosting; top it with the second layer.
4. Frost the top layer with the yellow frosting.
5. Attach a large ribbon or length of fabric to make the medal's neckpiece.
6. Write the words "Happy Birthday, Winner!" across the top of the cake.
7. Set tiny flags around the outside edge of the cake.

COSTUMES

- Have the kids dress in sweats, athletic outfits, or their favorite sports attire.
- Dress the party helpers as referees, in black-and-white-striped T-shirts and matching shorts.

DECORATIONS

- If you have any Olympic memorabilia, display it in the party room to set the mood.
- Hang up posters from around the world to give the party room an international atmosphere.

- Hang up posters of sporting events or favorite sports figures.
- Place sporting equipment on the party table as a centerpiece. Have fun by decorating the centerpiece with Ace-Bandages, Ben-Gay ointment, crutches, and so on.
- Fill the ceiling with helium balloons.
- Hang flags from other countries or states on the walls.
- Play Olympic music in the background to greet the guests.

GAMES

- Create a series of challenging games for the competing athletes, using the Olympic Games as a model. Include a relay race, a high jump, a weight-lifting contest, and a discus throw.
- Organize a decathlon. Have the kids perform ten different sports during the party—such as running, jumping, dancing, skating, swimming, biking, bowling, Ping-Pong playing, Frisbee throwing, and miniature golfing.
- Get some thick mats and have the kids do gymnastic stunts, following the lead of a gymnastic teacher.

- Have Silly Olympics, with such silly stunts as pie eating, wheelbarrow racing, clothes changing, feather-in-a-spoon carrying, Frisbee throwing, Hula-Hoop passing, or balloon popping.
- Divide the kids into two or three teams, and let them design the challenges for one another!

ACTIVITIES

- Make flags to represent each individual or team, using rectangles of white, fringed cloth attached to sticks or thin wooden dowels. Have the kids color the flags with fabric paint, permanent felt-tip pens, or puffy paints.
- Make T-shirts for the kids to wear during the events or create pennants to hang up while they compete.

VARIATIONS

- Take the kids to a sporting event and enjoy live-action athletics. Root for your team and eat ballpark food.
- Place penny bets on who will win, who will get hurt first, who will fall, and so on.

HELPFUL HINTS

- Try to include some cooperate games, or group games, so everyone wins.
- Be sure to have medals for all the kids, so that everyone takes home a prize.

FOOD

- Serve long, hearty hero sandwiches that the kids can cut to size
- For snacks, give the kids fruit bars, granola bars, or other healthy treats.
- Offer the kids Gatorade or other athletic drinks to quench their thirst.

FAVORS

- Send the athletes home with Frisbees, balls, Hula-Hoops, or other inexpensive sporting equipment.
- Give the kids pictures of famous athletes or sports-team banners, flags, or T-shirts.

PETS ON PARADE PARTY

Host an animal-themed party, and treat the kids to an afternoon with their favorite dogs, cats, mice, and hamsters! Have the kids bring their real pets to the party— if you've got the courage—or have them bring stuffed pets for a make-believe Pets on Parade Party.

INVITATIONS

- Cut out pictures of dogs and cats and glue them onto homemade cards. Draw speech balloons and have the animals invite the kids and their pets to the party.
- Send a snapshot of your dog or cat to each child, with the party details written on the back.
- Ask the kids to bring their stuffed animals (or real pets—as long as they're in cages!) to the party.

COSTUMES

- Tell the kids to come dressed as their favorite animals.
- Award prizes for creative costumes, with such categories as cutest, fuzziest, funniest, most vicious-looking, and so on. Make sure that everyone gets a prize.

DECORATIONS

- Place stuffed animals around the room.
- Make animal-shaped balloons and hang them from the ceiling.
- Cut out pictures of animals and use the pictures to decorate the tablecloth, place settings, and front door.
- Play animal songs or sounds for background music to welcome your guests.

GAMES

- Play Animal Bingo. Draw one extra-large bingo card on tagboard. Draw a grid of squares, and fill each square with the name or picture of an animal. Copy the bingo card onto sturdy paper, enough for all guests. On individually cut-up squares, write or draw the same animals. Hand out the Animal Bingo squares, call out the animals as you

pick them from the card pile, and have the kids set dog biscuits or cat treats onto the matching bingo squares. The first player to get five in a row across, down, or horizontally wins a pet toy!

ACTIVITIES

- Have the kids sit in a circle and make animal noises one at a time, while the other kids guess the animal.
- Have the kids act out an animal, without making any sounds, while the other kids guess the animal.
- Play Make-a-Critter. Fold a large sheet of white construction paper in half and then in half again. Unfold the paper, and spread it out on the table. Give the kids crayons or felt-tip pens. Have one kid draw an animal head in the top rectangle of the paper. When the kid finishes, fold back the top rectangle so it's hidden from view, and only the three remaining rectangles show. Then pass the paper to the left, and have that kid draw the body and arms of an animal in

the next rectangle. Repeat, having the kids draw legs in the third rectangle, and feet in the fourth rectangle. When they've finished, unfold the paper to see what new animal the kids have created. If you like, pass around more than one piece of paper at the same time, so the kids can create a whole bunch of new animals.

DOG BONE CAKE

1. Bake a loaf cake and four cupcakes; cool.
2. Set two cupcakes on each end of the loaf to make a dog bone shape.
3. Frost the loaf and the cupcakes with chocolate frosting.
4. Write a dog biscuit logo across the top.

FOOD

- Give the kids animal crackers as a snack.
- Make animal sandwiches cut with animal-shaped cookie cutters.
- Make cookies cut to look like dog biscuits.
- Serve make-believe animal food, such as tuna "cat food," cereal "dog food," Goldfish crackers "fish food," and so on.

FAVORS

- Give the kids anything for a pet: fur brushes, fancy collars or tags, chew toys, pet snacks, and so on.
- Have the kids take home the dishes they decorated during the party.
- Give the kids small books about dogs, cats, and other pets.

VARIATIONS

- Take the kids to a dog or cat show to see all the fancy breeds and fluffy tails.
- Go to a movie or rent a video that features an animal, such as a talking pig, an animated mouse, or a cartoon bear.

HELPFUL HINT

- Ask the kids to bring their animals in cages, so the cats and dogs don't fight or require lots of attention.

- Give each kid a plastic dog/cat dish. Have them write their pets' names on the dishes and decorate them on the outside with permanent felt-tip markers, paint, and other decorative materials. (Don't use glitter, though. If the pets will use the dish, the glitter may come off and get onto the food.)

PIRATE SHIP PARTY

Sail off to Pirate's Cove for a hearty party aboard ship. All you need are cardboard boxes and paint to turn your party place into a pirate ship! Yo-ho, yo-ho, it's a Pirate Ship Party for us!

INVITATIONS

- Help your guests find their way to Pirate's Cove with a Treasure Map invitation. Draw a simple map of your neighborhood, including the homes of each guest and your own. Mark your home with an X, then add familiar sights, and give them creative names, such as Hangman's Tree, Dead Man's Mall, and Peg-Leg's Restaurant. Photocopy the map and personalize each map by making a dotted-line path from the guest's house to the party house. Tear or burn the edges, roll the maps into scrolls, secure with gold strings, and mail.

TREASURE CHEST CAKE

1. Bake a rectangular cake; cool.
2. Frost with chocolate frosting. Decorate with colorful sprinkles and chocolate gold coins to make it look like a chest lid.
3. Clean the baking pan, then frost the outside sides of the pan.
4. Set the pan at a right angle to the cake to form a treasure chest.
5. Fill the chest with candy jewelry and chocolate gold coins.

- For fun, put the Treasure Map scrolls inside empty plastic soda bottles to create an Invitation in a Bottle. Hand deliver to guests. Let them figure out how to retrieve the invitations!
- Attach eye patches or plastic swords to the invitations.

DECORATIONS

- With a little imagination, you can turn the party area into a Pirate's Cove. Get a few large appliance boxes, and line them up to form the foundation of your pirate ship. Open the boxes at the top, and cut openings between connecting boxes to form sections of the ship. Cut out round windows along the sides. Form a "walk-the-plank" entrance by cutting an opening on one side of the ship and laying the cardboard piece on the floor. Bend the cardboard boxes into a point at both ends of the ship to form the fore and aft. Paint the whole ship brown, raise a crow's nest using a hat rack or an old lamp post, and attach a pirate flag. You're ready to sail!

GAMES

- Play Walk the Plank! Set out an eight-foot length of two-by-four board. Line the kids up at one end. Beginning with easy challenges, have the kids walk straight across the flat part of the board without stepping off into the "sea." After everyone has completed the first task, increase the difficulty level. Have the kids walk the plank backwards, sideways, hopping, without using their hands for balance, with weights on both arms to obscure balance, passing over an obstacle set in the middle, and—for the ultimate challenge—blindfolded! When a pirate falls into the sea, he or

COSTUMES

- Ask the kids to dress as pirates.
- Buy pirate-wear at a thrift store and let the kids dress up at the party.
- Provide eye patches and swords (see Activities), fake jewelry, handkerchiefs, and phony mustaches. Dot the kids' faces with black eye pencil to create "three-day beards."

she must drop out of the game. When only one pirate remains, award a prize.

- Have a Treasure Hunt. Hide some chocolate gold coins around the yard or party room, and let the kids hunt for them. Make sure everyone gets a handful of coins when the hunt is over.

ACTIVITIES

- Make eye patches for the pirates. Cut the eye patches from felt or imitation leather, and attach a length of elastic string on both sides.
- Make swords. Cut out short lengths of cardboard and round the tips. Cut two smaller pieces as the crossbars, and glue or staple the crossbars to the swords. Paint the blades silver and the handles black. Let the kids decorate their own swords.
- Make pirate flags. Give each kid a rectangular piece of lining material or cotton and permanent felt-tip pens. Let them color their own pirate flags. Staple the finished flags to dowels.

VARIATION

- Rent a pirate movie, such as *Peter Pan* or *Hook,* and have a video pirate party.

HELPFUL HINT

- Be sure to keep the homemade swords dull—no sharp points—and supervise the sword fights.

FOOD

- Serve bowls of hot soup to warm up the pirates, and call it Black Bart Stew.
- Offer plates of chicken legs or hot dogs, and let the kids eat with their fingers, the way pirates used to do.
- For a perfect pirate meal, serve fish 'n' chips!
- Let the pirates quench their thirst with apple cider.

FAVORS

- Send the pirates home with their loot— chocolate gold coins, eye patches, swords, costume parts, flags, and fake jewelry.

PJ PARTY

If you want to host a PJ Party—day or night—all your guests need is sleepwear! Once they're dressed for bed, keep them wide awake with lots of sleepytime games and activities!

INVITATIONS
- Photocopy and cut out pictures of your guests, using a yearbook or snapshots borrowed from parents. Fold construction paper into a side-fold card. Open the card and place a cut-out head near the top, leaving room for a body. Dress the body in pajamas by cutting out a pajama shape from a piece of flannel fabric and gluing it underneath the head. Close the card and cut out a hole in front to reveal the child's face. Write "You're invited..." on the outside of the card, and "...to a PJ Party!" on the inside, along with the party details. Mail to guests.

COSTUMES
- Ask your guests to dress in sleepwear—pajamas, long johns, robes, and slippers.
- Tell the guests that teddy bears, blankets, pillows, and other sleeping accessories are also welcome.

DECORATIONS
- Set up the party room to look like a giant sleeping area.
- Spread out mattresses, or cover the floor with sheets, blankets, and lots of pillows. Host the party right in the middle of the giant "bed."

- Keep the lights dim.
- Play lullabies for background music.
- Hang up pictures of people who are sleeping or are dressed in pajamas.
- Set teddy bears and other sleepy-time items around the party room.

GAMES
- Play the Slipper Game. Put all the guests' slippers into a pile. When you say "Go!" have the kids race to see who can locate and put on his or her slippers first.

- Play the Slipper Game again, but this time blindfolded. Have each guest, one at time, feel the slippers and try to guess which ones are his or hers.
- Play Hide the Slippers. Tuck the slippers into nooks and crannies around the party room. Let the guests try to find them in a kind of treasure-hunt game.
- Set out all the slippers in a row, and have the kids match the slippers to the guests.
- Have the kids close their eyes, pass the slippers around in a circle, and identify their owner just by feel.

ACTIVITIES

- Make Pillow Case Creations. Have the kids bring a plain white or lightly colored pillow case to the party, or provide them yourself. Set out felt-tip pens and puffy paints, and let the kids decorate the pillow cases.
- Tie-dye the pillow cases. Tie knots in the cases, dip the entire cases in fabric dye, untie the knots, and dry the cases in the dryer.

CEREAL PILLOW CAKE

1. Bake a rectangular cake; cool.
2. Cover the cake with fluffy white frosting so it looks like a soft pillow.
3. Crush a cup or two of colorful sweetened cereal, such as Trix or Fruit Loops, and sprinkle over the Pillow Cake.

FOOD

- Have a Breakfast Buffet any time of the day, by offering a variety of cereals and breakfast foods. Let the kids choose what they want to eat.
- Serve hot chocolate in coffee mugs to wash down breakfast.

VARIATIONS

- Choose another fashion theme for your party. For example, have a Fashion Mistake Party, where the kids come dressed in clothes they hate or bought by mistake; a Grunge Gear Party, where the kids wear their grungiest clothes; a Parent's Closet Party, where the kids wear something from mom's or dad's closet; or a Baby Clothes Party, where the kids choose something a baby might wear.
- Take the kids out to a coffee shop for a midday breakfast—still dressed in their pajamas!

HELPFUL HINT

- Warn the kids to dress warmly enough, and to bring a robe and extra socks just in case.

FAVORS

- Send the sleepyheads home with tiny teddy bears.
- Give the kids new toothbrushes to use at home.
- Hand out small pillows or pairs of sleep socks to go with the kids' pj's

PLANET EARTH PARTY

Celebrate the planet with a Planet Earth Party. Combine science, nature, and creativity, and you'll find a world full of curious fun and games!

INVITATIONS

- Send postcards of the planet earth, with the party details as the message.
- Make your own postcards by attaching magazine pictures of earth to index cards.
- Attach small plastic globes to the invitations, and mail them in small, recyclable boxes. (Globes are available at toy stores.)
- Write the party details on packets of flower or vegetable seeds using a black, permanent, felt-tip pen; mail to your guests.

FLOWER CAKE

1. Bake a sheet cake; cool.
2. Frost the cake with chocolate frosting.
3. Sprinkle crushed chocolate cookies on the frosting to look like dirt.
4. Top the cake with real or artificial flowers that appear to "grow" out of the cake. (If using real flowers, use edible varieties available at many grocery and specialty stores.
5. Add a few Gummy worms for even more fun!

COSTUMES

- Ask the kids to come dressed as scientists, explorers, or naturalists.
- Provide the kids with camouflage shirts or neckties, and men's large, old, white shirts for lab coats.
- Ask the kids to come dressed as something from the earth itself—and leave the costumes to their imaginations!

GAMES

- Have a Painted Snail Race. Ask the kids to "borrow" some snails from the yard. Give the kids poster paints and tiny brushes and have them decorate the snails' shells. Then line up the snails and set them free to race. The snail that crosses the finish line first wins a prize for its temporary owner. When the race is finished, return the snails to the yard.
- Have a Litter Race. Divide the kids into teams and give each team a paper bag. Give the kids a ten-minute time limit to collect as much litter in the neighborhood as they can. When all the kids return, count or weigh the litter, and award a prize.

ACTIVITIES

- Make a Tiny Terrarium. Save large, clear, plastic soda pop bottles—you'll need one for each guest. Cut the tops off the bottles, leaving about five inches on the bottom. Discard the tops. Give the kids the plastic bottoms, and have them fill the bottles with dirt and plant seeds. Or have the kids layer tiny rocks or sand in the bottoms to create earth's layers. Provide small plastic figures and tiny artificial plants to create miniature scenes.
- Create colorful sand designs. Color the sand by placing sand in bowls and rubbing the sand in each bowl with colored chalk—each bowl a different color. The chalk will disintegrate, coloring the

DECORATIONS

- Decorate the party room with posters of the earth, the stars, the environment—anything that has to do with the planet.
- Hang stars from the ceiling, cut out trees from construction paper and tape them to the walls, and draw a mural of the horizon.
- Set out globes of the earth, charts and maps, aerial photographs, and other views of our world.

sand. Have the kids pour the colored sand in layers. Finish by decorating the sand with artificial flowers.

• Make pressed flowers. Give each kid a flower, a thick book, and two sheets of wax paper. Have them place one sheet of wax paper into the middle of the open book. Tell them to place the flower on top of the wax paper and to arrange the petals any way they like. Then have them carefully place the second sheet of wax paper over the flower and close the book. Leave the flower in the book for at least thirty minutes before removing it.

• Create decorative flower pots. Give each guest a plastic pot, fabric scraps, glitter, stickers, ribbons, and puffy paints. Let the kids decorate their pots.

VARIATIONS

• Take the kids on a nature walk and point out environmental issues, topics, activities, and so on.
• Visit a museum and have the tour guide talk about the environment.

HELPFUL HINT

• Don't turn the party into a work day—keep it fun and interesting, while learning to keep the earth clean and healthy.

FOOD

• If you aren't up for escargot, offer the kids foods from the garden—carrot and celery sticks, zucchini wheels, cherry tomatoes, broccoli flowers, and so on.
• Have the kids make funny animals out of fruit and vegetables, using toothpicks to hold the pieces together. When they finish, they can eat their creations.
• Offer a veggie dip or fruit yogurt to go with the garden goodies.
• Make fruit shakes.

FAVORS

• Give the kids packets of flower or vegetable seeds to take home and plant.
• Offer gardening tools wrapped with ribbon.
• Have the kids take home the pressed flowers and flower pots they made.

PREHISTORIC PARTY

A Prehistoric Party comes together faster than you can say Tyrannosaurus Rex! Step into the past, where dinosaurs roamed the party room, and watch the megamonsters come to life!

INVITATIONS

- Buy large plastic eggs from a hobby or toy store. Cut out pictures of dinosaurs from children's coloring books, and write the party details on the backs. Enclose the pictures inside the plastic eggs, along with small egg candies. Decorate the eggs with permanent felt-tip pens or puffy paints. Hand deliver or mail the invitations in small padded boxes.
- Make pop-up invitations that look like eggs, with surprise baby dinosaurs inside. Fold a white sheet of paper in half, and cut out an egg shape, leaving one end of the egg connected. Cut out a small dinosaur picture to fit inside the egg. Fold the dinosaur in half, glue the bottom of the dinosaur to the inside bottom of the egg and the top of the dinosaur to the inside top of the egg. When you open the egg, the dinosaur will unfold. Write the party details around the dinosaur. Mail.

COSTUMES

- Have the kids come dressed as prehistoric people, cave dwellers, archeologists, or dinosaurs.

- Give the kids sheets of colored crepe paper, and let them design their own dinosaur costumes at the party.
- Offer the kids props to go with their costumes, such as scientific tools for the archeologists and bones for the cave people.

DECORATIONS

- Hang up large pictures or posters of dinosaurs.
- Make a volcano from large sheets of construction paper. Hang it on the wall.
- Set out dry ice to give the room a prehistoric feeling.

• Arrange the furniture in a circle. Drape old sheets and blankets over the furniture to create a cave. Let the kids eat and play games inside the megacave.

GAMES

• Play Archeologist. First, mix two cups of sand, one cup of cornstarch, and one and a half cups of water in a large pan on the stove. Heat the mixture until warm, then shape a handful of the mixture into an egg around a small plastic dinosaur. Allow the egg to dry until firm. Make one egg for each guest, and hide the eggs in the yard or party room. Let the explorers hunt for the eggs and break open their discoveries when they find them!

DINOSAUR CAKE

1. Bake a rectangular cake; cool.
2. Cut the cake in half lengthwise, and lay one half onto a serving plate.
3. Using a zigzag cut, slice the remaining half into two large triangles and a number of small triangles to form dinosaur head, tail, and spikes.
4. Place the spikes on top of whole half, and place large triangles at the head and tail.
5. Frost the cake with green or chocolate frosting. Use sprinkles and candy to create details for face, feet, and tail. Serve to carnivores.

• Have an archeological dig. Buy a plastic skeleton, available at science and toy stores, lay the skeleton out on the patio or other surface, and cover with dirt or sand. Provide the kids with brushes, and let them gently brush away the dirt or sand to discover the "fossil." Have them determine what it is.
• Play Bone Hunt. Distribute plastic skeleton bones throughout the party room, and let the kids hunt for them. When they find all the pieces, have them work as a team to put the skeleton back together!

FOOD

- Make Dinosaur Jell-O Eggs. Cut off the top of an egg, pour it out, and rinse the shell. Make enough for all the guests. Insert a small edible dinosaur or other critter into each shell. Mix Jell-O according to package directions, and pour into the egg shells. Cool the filled eggs in the refrigerator. After the Jell-O sets, have the kids crack the eggs open and eat the surprise inside. (Warn the kids to eat carefully, because the Jell-O contains a surprise.)
- Make Deep Sea Jell-O. Mix blue-colored gelatin, pour it into an aquarium bowl or a large clear bowl, and add Gummy fish. Allow to set, then serve.

FAVORS

- Create archeology kits by filling small boxes with compasses, paint brushes, freeze-dried food, rulers, and other scientific items, so the kids can make discoveries at home.
- Give the kids plastic dinosaurs or books about dinosaurs.

ACTIVITIES

- Make a giant dinosaur in the backyard. Have the kids shape a dinosaur using chicken wire. If throwing this party for younger children, create the dinosaur yourself before the kids arrive. Then let the kids cover the chicken wire with crepe paper to form a dinosaur's body.
- Cut out large dinosaur shapes from a cardboard box, one for each guest. Let the kids paint their shapes using poster paint. Have a dinosaur parade.

VARIATION

- Take the kids to a museum that features dinosaur exhibits.

HELPFUL HINT

- Handle the Jell-O dinosaur eggs carefully so they don't break before the Jell-O sets!

RESTAURANT/CAFÉ PARTY

Open your own restaurant for the day, and invite hungry patrons to come and dine in your one-of-a-kind eatery. With a little imagination you can turn your dining room into a diner, your kitchen into a café, or your party room into a pizza parlor. What's on the menu? Fun!

INVITATIONS
- Make homemade menus. Instead of food items, write the party details inside.
- If your party has a diner theme, copy a diner menu and add party details under the food listings.
- If your party theme is a French café, add a few French words to the party details.
- If your party theme is a high-school cafeteria, print your menu on the back of a school notice.
- If you prefer, write your party details on fancy or cartoon napkins; mail to guests.

MENU CAKE
1. Bake a sheet cake; cool.
2. Frost the cake with white frosting.
3. Write the name of your restaurant at the top of the cake, and add menu selections with frosting tubes.
4. Name the restaurant and each of the food selections after one of the guests, such as Sammy's Sherbet or Zack's Zucchini Squares.

COSTUMES
- Have your guests dress in a style appropriate to your restaurant theme:
  —For a fifties diner, have the kids dress in fifties style, with jeans and leather jackets or poodle skirts and cardigan sweaters.
  —For a French café, have the kids dress in their best clothes.
  —For a high-school cafeteria, the kids should dress like teenagers.

—For a high-school cafeteria, decorate the room in school colors, put up banners and pennants, feature your school mascot as the waiter, and play the school song.

- Choose another theme, such as a fancy restaurant, a pizza parlor, a California fern bar, a fast-food drive-through, an ethnic restaurant, such as Chinese or Indian, or a hotel banquet.

GAMES

No food fights, but you can have fun with food while waiting to be served.

- Play Read the Menu. Read the ingredients to popular meals, and have the kids guess what meals they make. For example, the combination of "hamburger, catsup, onions, and bread crumbs" makes meat loaf.
- Offer appetizers from different countries, and have the kids guess the ingredients—and the country of origin.
- Have a Taste Test with all kinds of strange things to sample. Blindfold the guests and have them identify what they're eating.

DECORATIONS

- Pick your favorite restaurant style and decorate the room accordingly:
  —For a fifties diner, decorate with lots of records, old photos, and letter sweaters, and play old rock and roll tunes.
  —For a French café, put up French posters and flags, and play French music.

ACTIVITY

- Give the kids a collection of appetizer ingredients, and ask them to make creatures using the provided ingredients. They can work in small groups or individually. Include such food items as variety crackers, cut-up vegetables and fruit, nuts and seeds, and bonding items, such as cream cheese, peanut butter, and other spreads. Award prizes for such categories as scariest, funniest, and so on.

FOOD

- Have your food suit the party theme to keep your restaurant authentic.

VARIATION

- Take the kids out to an unusual restaurant rather than eating at home. For example, go to a Japanese restaurant where you have to take your shoes off, a railroad restaurant where you eat inside individual train cars, a Moroccan restaurant where belly dancing is provided as entertainment, or an Indian restaurant where you eat only with your fingers.

HELPFUL HINT

- Be sure to check with parents regarding food allergies, so all the kids can enjoy the party without problems.

—At the diner, serve burgers, fries, shakes, and sodas.
—At the fancy restaurant, serve something French for the main course and something flaming for dessert.
—At the pizza parlor, serve pizza, naturally, and pour apple cider into beer mugs.
—At the high-school cafeteria? Mystery meat!

FAVORS

- Send the kids home with rolls of refrigerator cookie dough, so they can make dessert themselves.
- Give the guests recipes for special treats, along with nicely packaged appropriate ingredients.
- Hand out gift certificates to fast-food restaurants.

SAND CASTLE PARTY

Here's a weather-themed party that's perfect for summer. Or host it in the winter to warm yourselves up. Check out the Snow Sculpture Party for a year-round alternative!

INVITATIONS

- Cut out yellow suns from construction paper and write the party details on the suns in a circle. Place the suns in individual, sealable sandwich baggies, and add a little sand for fun.
- Mail postcards of the beach to get your guests in the mood for fun in the sun.

COSTUMES

- Have the kids wear bathing suits, shorts, tank tops, or Hawaiian shirts.
- Provide sunglasses, suntan lotion, beach hats, and other sunshine items.

DECORATIONS

- Set up a "beach" in the backyard by filling the sandbox with beach toys.
- Get the sprinklers going, and fill the kiddy pool for water games and fun.
- Make an ocean by cutting wave shapes out of blue construction paper and hanging them on the fence. Add tropical fish cutouts.
- Make a cardboard boat, and add lots of beach balls to create a party atmosphere.
- Play Hawaiian music in the background.

GAMES

- Host a Summer Olympics for your party games. (See Olympics Party.)
- Have swim races in the backyard pool or nearby lake.
- Do gymnastics on the lawn.
- Put together a track meet.

ACTIVITIES

- Let the kids make sand paintings with colored sand or salt. Tint sand or salt with colored chalk by rubbing colored chalk into a bowl of sand or salt.

- Have the kids fill baby food jars with colored sand to make rainbow layers.
- Make sand candles. Dig a hole in the sandbox, pour in wax, add a wick, and pull out a sand candle. Candle wax and wicks are available at craft and hobby stores.

FOOD

- Cut a watermelon in half, and scoop out the melon. Fill with frozen fruit balls (use the scooped-out melon to make melon balls).
- Fill a watermelon shell with raspberry sherbet, dot with chocolate chips to make "seeds," and serve a frosty watermelon dessert.

FAVORS

- Send the kids home with sand pails and shovels.
- Give the kids their own sunglasses.
- Hand out towels or beach hats.

SUNBURST CAKE

1. Bake one round cake and six cupcakes.
2. Set the cupcakes around the outside of the round cake to make rays.
3. Tint white frosting with yellow food coloring, and frost the cakes with yellow frosting.
4. Give the sun a face using decorator frosting tubes.

VARIATION

- Instead of hosting a sand castle party in the summer, have a make-believe summer party in the winter. Use your imagination to pretend it's cold when it's hot, and vice versa.

HELPFUL HINT

- If the weather won't cooperate, create your own realistic temperature in the party room. For a winter party, turn down the heat and turn on the air conditioner. For a summer party, turn up the heat and make it toasty inside.

SCIENCE EXPLORERS PARTY

Let the budding scientists enjoy a party that offers a close-up look at the wonders of the world. Science can be magical, tasty, silly, and fun when you create a few amazing experiments. Slip on the lab coats—it's time to explore the mysterious realms of weird science!

INVITATIONS

- Make invitations that appear right before your guests' eyes using this scientific experiment. Use paintbrushes or toothpicks to write the party details with milk on white paper. Tell your guests to heat the paper over a candle or in the oven, with adult supervision. The heat will reveal the invitation!
- Write the party information with a white crayon, then have the kids color over the paper with another crayon to reveal the secret message.

COSTUMES

- Buy some men's white shirts at a thrift store, and use them as lab coats for your guests. Write their scientist names on one pocket, such as Dr. Frankenstein or Dr. Schweitzer, with a permanent felt-tip pen.
- Offer the kids goofy glasses and wild ties to go with their outfits, and tuck some pens into their pocket protectors.

DECORATIONS

- Place jars full of colored water on the table, and run hoses from one jar to another to look like experiments.
- Set dry ice in the center of the table so the steam creates a weird bubbling experiment.
- Cut out question marks from black construction paper, and tape them to the walls or hang them from the ceiling with string.
- Borrow microscopes, chemistry sets, magnifying glasses, compasses, and so on, and place them on the table and all around the party room.

GAMES

- Before the party, take close-up pictures of everyday items. Develop the pictures, glue them onto colored construction paper, and draw a magnifying glass around each picture, so they look as though they are being viewed through a magnifier. Have the kids examine the pictures and try to guess what everyday items are represented. Since the items have been enlarged, identifying them should be a challenge.

ACTIVITIES

- Use a child's chemistry set to do some science experiments.
- Make Slime for the kids to enjoy. Mix 2 cups of white glue and 1½ cups of water in a large bowl. Add a few drops of food coloring. In a separate container, dissolve 2 teaspoons of Borax in ⅔ cup warm water; mix well. Combine the Borax solution with the glue solution and watch what happens to the mixture. Distribute to the kids for exploration. Tell the kids not to eat the Slime!

COMPASS CAKE

1. Bake two round cakes; cool.
2. Cover one cake with frosting, top with second cake, and frost the entire cake with white frosting.
3. Using a frosting tube, draw a compass face onto the cake, marking north, south, east, and west.

FOOD

- Have a Popcorn Volcano Eruption. Spread out a large clean sheet on the floor and have the kids sit outside the edge. Set a popcorn maker in the center, and prepare popcorn according to directions. Do NOT put the lid on the popcorn maker! Watch the "volcano" erupt and shoot "hot lava" all over the sheet. Make sure everyone stays away from the popper while it's on, so the kids don't get sprayed with hot oil or kernels.
- Cut celery stalks and set them in glasses of water tinted with food coloring. Let the celery stalks soak up the

colored water, remove them from the glasses, and serve to the kids with cream cheese or peanut butter.

FAVORS

- Send the scientists home with magnets, compasses, bug collectors, magnifying glasses, kaleidoscopes, or the ingredients for Slime.
- Give the kids small books on famous scientists.
- Offer the kids easy-to-do scientific experiments to take home.

VARIATIONS

- Instead of having the party at home, take the scientists on a nature walk and discover new life forms.
- Head for the museum and explore the world of dinosaurs, early man, or other science-related adventures.
- Instead of a Compass Cake, make a Rock Cake. Bake a chocolate cake filled with nuts and marshmallows, cover with chocolate frosting, and top with "rock" candy.

HELPFUL HINT

- Tell the kids that experimenting with science can be dangerous, and warn them to use caution and adult supervision when exploring.

SCREEN TEST PARTY

The stars will shine bright for your Screen Test Party. Give your actors a script and a costume, and watch them light up the stage. Set up the lights, turn on the camera, and you'll have plenty of action.

INVITATIONS

- Cut out star shapes from silver tagboard and write the party details on the backs. Mail to guests in envelopes filled with confetti stars and covered with star stickers.
- Photocopy a picture of each guest, have the pictures enlarged at a copy store, cut them into star shapes, and write the party details on the backs.
- Take pictures of a completed party invitation and develop into negatives. Cut up the strip of negatives into individual clips, and place a clip into each envelope. Have each guest develop the negative into a picture to read the invitation.

HOLLYWOOD STAR CAKE

1. Bake two square cakes; cool.
2. Cut off all four corners on one of the cakes.
3. Place the corners at the sides of the other cake to form a star.
4. Frost the cake.
5. Serve ice cream bonbons with each slice.

COSTUMES

- Ask the guests to come dressed as favorite movie or television stars.
- Assign the kids particular stars, to match the script you'll provide.
- Provide sunglasses for each star.

DECORATIONS

- Set the stage for a screen test. Create a platform on which the kids can perform and cover the platform with flooring or carpeting. Hang a drape behind the platform to create a stage. Prop up the video camera and hook up a television monitor nearby. Add construction paper signs to give the atmosphere of a sound stage. Write such phrases as "Quiet on the set" and "Do not enter when camera light is on."
- Play movie tunes for background music.

GAMES

- Get popular-movie scripts from your local library or a college theater department. Pull out excerpts, and have the kids take turns reading the lines. Have the other guests try to name the movie and the actor who originally said the lines.
- Have the kids silently act out favorite movie scenes. See if the other guests can identify the scenes.
- Play a game of Charades acting out only movie titles.

ACTIVITIES

- Take the kids aside one at a time and videotape them doing the same dramatic scene. Don't let the other guests see the screen tests while they are being performed. After everyone has done the scene, gather the group together as an audience and have them view the screen tests.
- Videotape a scene that involves all the guests at once, and play it back for the kids to watch.

VARIATIONS

- Videotape the party. At the end of the party, gather the audience together and watch the "outtakes"— all the candid scenes that occurred during the party.
- Make a musical lip-sync tape, and have the kids reenact *Grease* or *Annie.*
- Let the kids perform anything they want, from a guitar solo to a dance routine.

HELPFUL HINTS

- If any of the kids are camera shy, cover the "on" light with tape—they may forget the camera is running.
- Give the kids costume accessories to enhance their outfits and help them get into their roles more easily.
- Try to have equal parts for all the performers, so everyone is a "star."

FOOD

- Serve popcorn while you watch the performances.
- Offer the kids typical theater candy— Jujubes, Jordan Almonds, Raisinettes.
- Make a dish that is typical of the script, such as marshmallow treats for *Ghostbusters* or fruit dinosaurs for *Jurassic Park.*

FAVORS

- Send the kids home with Polaroid snapshots of themselves acting out their scenes.
- Give the kids inexpensive videotapes of favorite old movies.
- Hand out plastic sunglasses, movie posters, or star magazines.

SECRET AGENT PARTY

Go undercover for this top-secret party. The event is full of surprises, as the secret agents try to figure out what's going on! Put on your trench coats and pull down your hats—you don't want anyone to see you having this much fun!

INVITATIONS
- Write the invitation in code and send it to the spy recruits. Send the decoder the next day—give the spies a day to decode the invitations on their own. After the code is broken, have the guests call and give a coded RSVP.
- If you don't hear from one or two guests, send them a note telling them how to solve the mysterious message.

COSTUMES
- Have the kids come dressed as their favorite spies, such as James Bond, Inspector Gadget, Harriet the Spy, Inspector Hound, and others.
- When the guests arrive, present them with spy kits—a notepad, a magnifying glass, a pair of plastic glasses and nose, and a code book to use throughout the party.
- Give each kid a code name and a phony passport.

DECORATIONS
- Drape the room in sheets to create secret hiding places for the spies.

- Have the kids give a password at the door. Revealed the password, along with a secret handshake, in the invitation.
- Talk in low voices.
- Play James Bond music in the background.
- Place cut-out question marks around the room to hide clues for a later game.

GAMES

- Play Eye Witness. Have an outsider run into the room, complete a fake crime, and escape. Ask the guests questions about what happened, and see how many good eye witnesses you have in the group.
- Have a Mystery Hunt. Hide spy items in the party room, such as a set of fingerprints, a photograph of a suspect, a mysterious message, and so on. Announce or stage a crime, and tell the kids to collect the evidence. When they have collected all the evidence, have them figure out the solution to the crime.
- Play Bomb Squad. Hide a ticking kitchen timer somewhere in the room, and have the kids try to find it before it "goes off."

ACTIVITIES

- Have the spies make their own spy kits. Include powder for making fingerprints, disposable cameras, magnifying glasses,

SECRET CODE CAKE

1. Bake a rectangular cake; cool.
2. Frost the cake with chocolate or white frosting.
3. Write a message in code on top of the cake in a contrasting color of frosting.
4. Hide the cake so the spies have to find the dessert before they can solve the puzzle on top. Give them clues to the code.

VARIATIONS

- Take the kids to see a spy movie, then act out some of the scenes when you get home.
- Rent a James Bond video and enjoy the show with bags of homemade popcorn.

HELPFUL HINT

- Buy a few old brown shirts at a thrift store in case some of the kids don't have spy costumes.

decoders, and some puzzles, such as a box with a secret compartment.
- Divide the kids into two teams and have each team create a puzzle for the other team to solve. Have the puzzles include treasure hunts.

FOOD

- Have a mystery meal with one "poison" item for the kids to detect. Serve lots of little sandwiches with a variety of fillings, and spread one with a distinct flavoring, such as curry, garlic, or other spice. Hand out the sandwiches and see if the spies can tell which sandwich has been "poisoned."

FAVORS

- Send the kids home with spy kits, magnifying glasses, *Harriet the Spy* books, plastic glasses with nose disguises, and disposable cameras.

SLEEPWALKING PARTY

Instead of a daytime party, host a nighttime party and have the guests spend the night! They get to wear their pajamas, bring their pillows and sleeping bags, and enjoy an evening of scary stories, silly stunts, midnight snacks, and sudden surprises!

INVITATIONS

- Color postcards with bright yellow crayon, then cover with black poster paint. Scratch off star shapes in the paint using the end of a paper clip. The stars will shine through the black paint to look like a night sky. Write the party details on the backs; mail to guests.
- Send the kids toothbrushes with party details written in permanent felt-tip pen on the handles. They can use the toothbrushes in the morning!
- Ask the kids to bring sleeping bags and pillows to the party, if necessary.

COSTUMES

- Have the kids wear pajamas, and tell them to bring robes and slippers.
- Ask the kids to create new fashions using their pajama clothing. Award prizes for most creative, silliest, most daring, most bizarre, and so on.
- Give the kids nightcaps to wear.
- Have the kids bring a toy to sleep with.

DECORATIONS

- Cut out paper stars, planets, and moons from construction paper, and hang them from the party room ceiling, to create an outdoors-under-the-stars feel.
- Light the room with flashlights instead of regular lights, or hang Christmas lights around the room.
- Spread sleeping bags all over every inch of the floor.
- Play lullaby songs in the background to set the mood.

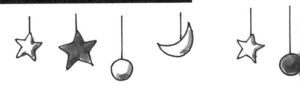

GAMES

- Play the Robe Game. Pair up the kids and have one player in each pair put on a robe. Have the pairs hold hands. The person wearing the robe must try to remove it and get it onto the second person, without letting go of his or her hands.
- Play Blanket Ball. Spread out a blanket and have all the guests stand around the edge of the blanket and hold a piece of it. Toss a ball into the center, and have the players keep the ball bouncing by moving the blanket up and down. (You may want to do this outside. If not, remove all breakables!)
- Play Slipper Scramble. Have everyone put a slipper into a pile in the middle of the room. When you say, "Go!" players must scramble to find their slipper and put it on. Try the game again in the dark.

ACTIVITIES

- Have the kids do each other's hair and makeup.
- Tell ghost stories or watch a scary video.
- Play board games.
- Design new sleepwear fashions.
- Have a pillow fight.
- Play Truth or Dare. Have everyone confess to a secret in answer to a question. Those who don't confess have to face the consequences, such as "Sing opera," "Dance the twist," or "Count backwards from 100."
- Tie a ribbon to the toes of the kids who fall asleep, and connect the ribbon to other sleepy toes in the room.

BEDDY-BYE CAKE

1. Bake a sheet cake; cool.
2. Frost the cake with tinted frosting.
3. Use frosting tubes, sprinkles, and candy to replicate your child's bedspread.
4. Add pillows using marshmallows.

FOOD

- Serve midnight snacks—chips and cookies, pizza, milk shakes, muffins—almost anything you want.
- Make a giant pancake in the morning. Fill it with fruit and serve with whipped cream and a cherry.
- Whip up omelets in the middle of the night, made to order.

FAVORS

- Send the kids home with personalized toothbrushes, scrunchies for their hair, little teddy bears, or night-lights.
- Get the kids scary books to read in bed at night, such as *Goosebumps,* or books of funny poetry, such as *Poetry Party* by Bruce Lansky.

VARIATIONS

- Instead of having an overnighter, have a daytime slumber party. Ask the guests to wear pajamas to the party, then do all the things you would do at a slumber party—except sleep.
- Take everyone out to a restaurant for breakfast in their pajamas!

HELPFUL HINTS

- Set a deadline for the party fun, and have the kids get some sleep so they aren't too tired the next day.
- Let the kids sleep in the next morning, then make a hearty breakfast and send them on their way.

SNOW SCULPTURE PARTY

If it's cold outside, host a Snow Sculpture Party, with decorations provided by Mother Nature! Bundle up, head outside, and create your own show in the snow.

INVITATIONS

- Design one-of-a-kind invitations from paper doilies. Make personalized snowflakes for each of your guests. Write the party details on the doilies, fold, and mail to your guests.
- Send the kids pictures of snow scenes, to get them in a frosty mood for the party. Write the party details on the backs.

COSTUMES

- Ask the guests to bundle up in ski clothes, warm-up suits, or long under-wear for your ice-cold adventure.
- Provide extra mittens, scarves, ear muffs, and so on, to cover the gaps.

SNOWMAN CAKE

1. Bake two round cakes, one larger than the other, and one cupcake; cool.
2. Line up the two cakes and the cupcake to make a snowman.
3. Frost the cake with white frosting, top with coconut, and add chocolate chip eyes, cherry lips, and other details with frosting tubes.

DECORATIONS

- Carve a snowman out of large chunks of Styrofoam.
- Make icicles from white paper folded into cone shapes, and hang them from the ceiling.
- Set dry ice on the party table for a frosty feel.
- Play "Frosty the Snowman" and other winter tunes in the background.

GAMES

- Sock-skate on a freshly waxed kitchen floor.
- Have a luge race down a snowy hill on a sled, or on a grassy hill on cardboard.

FOOD
- Make snowballs by scooping out balls of vanilla ice cream and rolling them in flaky coconut.
- Make your own snow cones using real snow. Get a scoop of snow, pour some juice on top, and eat. If you don't have snow, make some by whirling ice in a blender.
- Make penguins by cutting open dates, filling with cream cheese to make tummies, and adding tiny cheese triangles for beaks and feet.
- Warm up the kids with mugs of steaming cocoa.

FAVORS
- Offer ice-cream coupons the kids can cash in later.
- Give the kids funny mittens to wear home.
- Hand out Popsicle forms to take home.

ACTIVITIES
- Let the kids carve their own snow people from Styrofoam.
- Have the kids make individual ice-cream sculptures. They can eat their works of art.
- Create "snowstorms" in a jar. Fill baby food jars with ivory snowflakes and water. Glue a winter scene or snowman on the inside lid, and allow to dry. Replace the lid, shake the jar, and watch the snow fall.
- Make "snowballs" out of waded up white paper, cotton balls, or balled white socks. Toss them around the room. (Make sure to remove all breakables.)

VARIATIONS
- In the summer, host the party in the house. Turn up the air conditioner to create winter weather.
- Instead of a Snow Sculpture Party, have a sand castle party in the winter. (See Sand Castle Party.)

HELPFUL HINT
- Make sure that the kids don't get too chilled in the cold.

SPACE INVADERS PARTY

Take a trip to outer space while the fares are still cheap! Venture to the Black Hole, the Milky Way, the planet Mars, and maybe take a ride on the Starship Enterprise, as you make your way through the stratosphere. Fasten your seat belts, it's going to be a bumpy ride!

INVITATIONS

- Design the invitations to look and read like tickets for a Space Shuttle ride from the NASA launch site, which just happens to be your house. Mail tickets to passengers, along with boarding passes, baggage claims, and home-made brochures of the destination.
- Send the guests star charts to guide them to your home planet—the Planet Party!
- Enclose a package of glow-in-the-dark stars, or make your own with glow-in-the-dark paint and cardboard cutouts.

MOON CAKE

1. Bake or buy an angel food cake.
2. Cover the cake with fluffy white frosting or whipped cream.
3. Top the frosting with chunks of hon-eycomb candy to look like volcanic moon rocks.
4. Place a small United States flag in the center of the cake to claim the territory.

COSTUMES

- Ask your guests to dress appropriately for the space ride—*Star Trek* costumes, *Flash Gordon* fashions, even space monsters styles.
- Give the kids doodle-bug headbands or homemade masks of favorite space characters.
- Make phasers from tagboard and pin them on the guests as they arrive.

- Hang posters of the planets and other space charts on the walls.
- Play *Star Trek* videos or music in the background.

GAMES

- Play Space Exploration. Divide your guests into two teams and give each team a skein of yarn. Send the teams to different parts of the house or yard, and have them wind the yarn around various pieces of furniture or plants, to create a maze. Have one group try to follow the yarn path through space. If anyone lets go, they will be lost in space forever. When one team finishes, have the other team follow their yarn path.
- Have a Moon Rock hunt on your new planet. Paint rocks with glow-in-the-dark paint, and hide them around the room. Turn out the lights, then race to see who can collect the most moon rocks for a prize.

DECORATIONS

- Create your own universe in the party room by cutting out tagboard stars and painting them with glow-in-the-dark paint. Hang the stars from the ceiling with ribbon or string. Buy nine different-sized balls, paint them with iridescent paint, and hang them from the ceiling to recreate the planets.
- Use Christmas lights with white bulbs to illuminate the party area.

ACTIVITIES

- Make your own Stargazers. Have the kids bring oatmeal boxes. Paint the containers black, then poke holes in the bottoms in constellation shapes. Give each guest a flashlight, turn off the lights, and have the kids shine the flashlights into the containers. Aim the bottoms of the containers toward the ceiling. The room should light up with stars!
- Make Moon Walkers for a challenging trip over the new terrain. Have the kids bring

two coffee cans to the party. Paint the cans black, then poke holes near the bottom on either side. String ropes through the holes, leaving three-foot lengths on each side of the cans for the kids to hold. Turn the cans bottom up on the ground. Have the kids step up on the cans and hold onto the ropes. Then have them try to "walk" on the bumpy terrain using the Moon Walkers.

FOOD

- Go to a sports store and buy freeze-dried "astronaut" food. You can get packaged ice cream, just-add-water soups and stews, and lots of interesting space munchies.
- Make your own asteroid snack. Slice the bottom off a melon so it sits flat. Skewer fruit pieces with toothpicks and insert ends into the melon. Cover the melon with fruit spikes. Let the space invaders pull the skewers and eat the fruit.

VARIATIONS

- Visit a space museum and get a first-hand look at the latest from NASA.
- Have an astronaut visit the party and talk about what it's like to prepare for space travel.

HELPFUL HINT

- Tack up dark sheets along the walls to make the party room look dark and barren for your space exploration.

FAVORS

- Give the space explorers books about space.
- Offer freeze-dried food to take home.
- Give the kids glow-in-the-dark stars to put on their bedroom ceilings.
- Send the kids home with inexpensive classic space movies from the fifties.

SPANISH FIESTA PARTY

Head for the border as you host a Spanish Fiesta for your invited mehas and mehos. With colorful decorations, Mexican food, and festive music, you'll feel like you're in South America, just in time to celebrate Carnival!

INVITATIONS

- Write the party details on small red, white, and green Mexican flags made from construction paper. Place the flags in envelopes and mail to amigos.
- For fun, write the party details in Spanish, so the kids have to translate them to find out about the party.

COSTUMES

- Ask the kids to come dressed in Mexican, South American, or Spanish outfits.
- Provide the kids with sombreros, serapes, and sandals to add to their ensembles.
- Dress the kids in red, white, and green crepe paper when they arrive, creating individual Spanish fashions for each guest.

DECORATIONS

- Make large, colorful flowers from tissue paper, and set them all around the party room.
- Cover the party table in red, white, and green paper tablecloths. Add candles to light up the room.
- Hang a large piñata from the ceiling, and purchase or make several small piñatas to use as decorations around the room.
- Set out Mexican blankets, bowls, fans, trinkets, and other inexpensive decorations. Most are available at import stores.
- Give the room a festive outdoor patio look by making a canopy of crepe paper ribbons in the colors of the Spanish flag.
- Play Spanish music in the background for added atmosphere.

GAMES

• Play a version of the Mexican Hat Dance that's more fun and lively than the old-fashioned game. Blow up red, green, and white balloons, and attach them to ribbons or strings about two feet long. Gather the guests in the party room and tie a ribbon to each player's nondominant leg. When you say, "Go!" have the players try to stomp and pop each other's balloons. At the same time, they should try to keep anyone from popping their balloon!

• Play the game again, this time tying the balloons to each player's dominant leg, forcing the players to use their nondominant leg to pop the other player's balloons.

ACTIVITIES

• Make your own piñatas. They're easy to make when you follow this simple method. First, have each guest blow up a balloon. Tie off the balloons with string and set them on a table covered with

newspaper. Pour liquid starch into individual bowls; prepare one for each guest. Place colored tissue paper on the table and have the kids tear the paper into large pieces or strips. Have the kids dip a piece of tissue paper into the starch, then paste it onto their balloons. Repeat until the balloons are completely covered with several layers of tissue paper. Allow the balloons to dry in the sun. When dry, decorate them with funny or monster faces using permanent felt-tip pens.

• Make Baker's Clay jewelry. To make Baker's Clay, mix 4 cups of flour, 1 cup of salt, and 1½ cups of water, to make a dough. (Add more flour or water as needed, for a smooth, nonsticky consistency.) Let the kids shape the dough

---

SPANISH FLAG CAKE

1. Bake a rectangular cake; cool.
2. Frost the cake with red, white, and green frosting to replicate the Mexican flag.
3. Add colorful sugar or frosting flowers to the cake.
4. Decorate with small Spanish toys that the kids can take home.

FAVORS

- Send your amigos home with sombreros, panchos, or some castanets.
- Let the kids take home the large paper flowers you used for decoration.
- Give the kids Spanish picture books or cassette tapes of Spanish children's songs.
- Let the kids take home the piñatas they made.
- Have the kids take the Baker's Clay jewelry they made.

into beads, pendants, or charms. Use a skewer to make holes for string. Bake at 250 degrees for an hour, remove from heat, and set aside to cool. When cool, let the kids paint their creations with poster paint or acrylic paint. String with thick embroidery floss to make necklaces and bracelets.

FOOD

- Offer a make-it-yourself taco bar. Include such items as cooked ground beef, varieties of shredded cheese, chopped tomato, shredded lettuce, diced mild green chilies, chopped olives, sour cream, and salsa. Give the guests large heated taco shells and let them fill up!

VARIATIONS

- Take the kids to a Spanish bazaar, and let them taste the food and pick out small trinkets to buy.
- Treat the kids to lunch or dinner at a Spanish restaurant. Let them try something new.
- Ask a Spanish storyteller to come to your party and tell tales about life in Mexico, South America, or Spain.

HELPFUL HINTS

- Have an interpreter come to the party to translate everything from English to Spanish as the party unfolds.
- If any of your guests have relatives who are Spanish, Mexican, or South American, ask them for tips and suggestions to make the fiesta more authentic.

SPLISH-SPLASH PARTY

What's the only ingredient you need for a successful Splish-Splash party? Water! Watch the wet ones frolic in the surf and sun. If you don't live near the surf, make your own Water Wonderland right in the backyard. It's time to get wet!

INVITATIONS

- For a fascinating underwater invitation, use a permanent felt-tip pen to write the party details on a piece of colorful plastic, such as a cut-up beach ball or margarine tub lids. Insert the plastic invitation into a sealable lunch baggy. Fill the bag half-full with blue-tinted water (use blue food coloring). Add plastic or metallic confetti to make the water sparkle, then glue the bag shut with superglue. Allow to dry, then place in a small box and mail.

RAINBOW CAKE

1. Bake two round cakes; cool.
2. Cut the cakes in half crosswise.
3. Place all four halves together to form a large half circle, and frost the sides so they stick together.
4. Turn the cake onto its flat side, with the rounded side up.
5. Divide a can of white frosting into individual bowls, and tint each bowl a different color—to make the colors of the rainbow.
6. Frost the cake in rows to create a rainbow effect.

COSTUMES

- Have the kids come dressed in clothes they don't mind getting wet. Bathing suits are preferred, but it's sometimes fun to get wet in shorts and a T-shirt for a change.
- Ask the kids to bring beach towels, sunscreen, sunglasses, and hats.

any other fun water toys you have around the house.

- Don't forget the squirt guns, water pails, and sponges!

GAMES

- Have a Water War with squirt guns, wet sponges, and water pails. Give the kids pan lids so they can protect themselves from the onslaught.
- Create a Splash Machine. Have the kids line up, then pass buckets of water from person to person, and dump them into the kiddy pool. Watch the kids get all wet!
- Throw coins into the pool, and let the kids scramble for them.
- Toss a bunch of balloons into the kiddy pool, and let the kids try to pop the slippery balloons by sitting on them.
- Have a tug-of-war at the kiddy pool. Separate the kids into two teams, station them on opposite sides of the pool, and have each team try to pull the other team into the water using rope.
- Make a slippery slide on the lawn. Spread large plastic garbage bags over the grass, and attach a hose at one end.
- Play Snake in the Grass. Have one player turn the sprinkler on and off, without looking at the rest of the players. Have the other players run through the area where the sprinklers are. The player who first makes it from one end of the area to the other without getting sprayed wins.

DECORATIONS

- Host the party outside where the water is plentiful and you don't have to worry about making a mess.
- Cut out blue waves from construction paper, and tack them to the top of the fence, to give the feeling of being underwater.
- Get out the sprinklers with a variety of heads and hoses, the kiddy pool, and

ACTIVITIES

- Make your own Spongies to use in the pool or bathtub. Give the kids colored sponges, and let them cut the sponges into various shapes. Then let them take the sponges into the water to play, or have the kids use the sponges to paint with tempera paint on large sheets of paper.
- Fill the kiddy pool with water, and add ⅓ cup dishwashing liquid (Dawn works best) and 2 teaspoons glycerin; mix well. Twist metal coat hangers or pipe cleaners into shapes, and use them to create bubbles from the giant pool of solution. Warn the kids not to splash in the solution, since the soap will sting their eyes.

VARIATIONS

- Have the party at a lake or pool.
- If you have water slides nearby, spend a hot afternoon sliding your way to cool, wet fun.
- If it rains, rent *Flipper* or *Free Willie*, and watch the video while you picnic on beach towels in bathing suits.

HELPFUL HINTS

- Make sure everyone knows they're going to get wet at this wild party.
- Have the kids wear sunglasses to protect their eyes.
- Tell all the kids to use sunscreen.

FOOD

- Make Frozen Slushies. Fill paper cups with fruit juice and place them in the freezer for two hours. Remove and stir with a spoon. Return to the freezer for another half hour. Remove, stir again, and serve.
- Make Popsicles from fruit juice, and add a slice of fruit for fun.
- Fill hollow oranges with fruit juice, freeze, and serve as snacks.
- Serve watermelon slices.

FAVORS

- Send the kids home with new towels.
- Hand out squirt guns, water sponges, sand pails, water goggles, or fancy sprinkler heads.
- Give the kids bubble solution to take home.

SPORTS AND GAMES PARTY

Gather sports fans for an exciting sporting event based on your child's interests. Turn the backyard into a baseball park, a football field, even a hockey rink, with a little imagination.

INVITATIONS

- Create your own sporting event tickets by copying some authentic tickets from a favorite sport. Fill in the party details, and personalize each ticket for the invited fans.
- Write the party details on the backs of sports cards, so your guests can begin a collection.
- Make pennants from colored construction paper, and mail them in large envelopes to the fans. The kids can hang them on the walls until party time!

COSTUMES

- If you're hosting a baseball party, have the kids wear baseball uniforms. For a soccer party, have them dress in soccer gear. Whatever the party theme, ask the fans to dress appropriately for the "game."
- Have the kids dress as fanatical sports fans, cheerleaders, mascots, food vendors, coaches, umpires, or other sports figures.
- Make your own sports logo T-shirts, and give them to your guests to wear at the party.

DECORATIONS

- Fill the walls of your party room with sports memorabilia appropriate to the sport you select as your theme.
- Hang up pennants from various teams, posters of all-star players, jerseys, hats, and other sports-related items.
- Cover the table with a paper tablecloth made to look like a baseball diamond, football field, or other sports arena.
- Write each guest's name on a place mat, and assign each guest a number.
- Make a centerpiece out of funny sports items, such as an Ace Bandage, Ben-gay muscle ointment, a broken bat, some shredded balls, and so on.

- Place balls all over the party room to use for later games.
- Play "Jock Jams" or other sports-themed music during the party to add excitement and atmosphere.

GAMES

- Have a minigame in the backyard or park, and play baseball, football, soccer, or other favorite sport.
- Put on a triathlon and play twenty minutes of each game to keep the kids on their toes!
- Play Silly Sports. Base the game on a real sport, such as baseball, but have every player make up one silly rule for the new version. For example, rules for Silly Sport baseball may include the following: "All players must bat with one hand," "Pitcher must toss the ball from a sitting position," or "Base runners can only run backwards."

SPORTS CAKE

1. Bake a square or rectangular cake, depending on what type of sports field you select.
2. Frost the cake with white frosting for a hockey rink and green frosting for a football or baseball field.
3. Draw grid lines as needed.
4. Line up plastic players on the field, as though they're playing a game.

ACTIVITIES

- Hand out baseball cards, or other sports-related cards, and let the kids exchange them with one another.
- Make your own jerseys by using puffy paints on white T-shirts.
- Buy a cardboard cutout of a famous sports figure, and take Polaroid pictures of the kids standing with the pro.

• Make a Soccer Ball Snacker. Spear vegetables or fruits with toothpicks. Stick one end of the toothpick into a Styrofoam ball, and let the kids choose their snacks.

FAVORS

• Send the kids home with headbands that feature team logos.
• Give the kids baseball or football cards to trade.
• Offer pennants, posters, or statistic books about favorite sports teams.

VARIATIONS

• Take the kids to a sporting event and enjoy the live action and excitement.
• Instead of baseball or hockey, choose a more unusual sport as your party theme. For example, race car driving, horse racing, swimming, or bowling all make fun party themes.
• Watch a game on TV and make penny bets on all the things that might happen during the game.
• Invite a local athlete to visit your party and talk about what it's like to be a sports figure.

HELPFUL HINT

• Be ready with a backup plan in case it rains. For example, show a sports-related video, such as *Mighty Ducks* or *Major League.*

FOOD

• Make Rice Krispie Baseballs. First follow the Rice Krispie Treat recipe on the box. Then shape the mixture into balls, instead of pressing it into a pan. Serve with carrotstick or breadstick "bats."
• Make Jell-O hockey pucks by chilling grape Jell-O in muffin tins.
• Shape a cheese log into a football.

STORYBOOK PARTY

Make your child's favorite storybook come alive by turning your party room into a *Lion King* jungle, a *Little Mermaid* lagoon, or even a Dr. Seuss playground. For older kids, use chapter books based on *Babysitter's Club*, *Goosebumps*, or *Sweet Valley Twins*. Open the book and watch the party unfold!

INVITATIONS

* Photocopy the cover of a favorite book and white-out the title. Replace the title with the name of your party theme, then add the party details around the edge.
* Make your own small storybook from construction paper, and use it as an invitation.

COSTUMES

* Ask the kids to come dressed as characters from their favorite books.

STORYBOOK CAKE

1. Bake two rectangular cakes; cool.
2. Set the cakes side by side to look like an open book.
3. Frost both cakes with white frosting.
4. Write your party title and other inscriptions on the cakes with frosting tubes, to look like words on a page.
5. Place a piece of licorice between the two cakes to form a bookmark.

DECORATIONS

* Check out a bunch of books from the library and set them all over the party room.
* Choose a favorite book. Use construction paper to reproduce items and scenes found in the book. For example, you might draw large trees for a jungle, fish for under the sea, and so on.
* Ask the library for reading posters featuring books or famous people.

materials, and give the kids some ideas if they get stuck.
- Have a storyteller come to the party to tell some classic tales.
- Award prizes for costumes. Make sure everyone gets a prize by creating lots of winning categories, such as cutest, scariest, funniest, and most creative.

FOOD

- Choose foods from favorite stories, such as a jam sandwich from *The Giant Jam Sandwich*, or muffins and honey from a Winnie-the-Pooh story.

FAVORS

- Give each kid a Golden Book or a children's paperback book to take home and enjoy.
- Laminate special homemade bookmarks, or buy some from a bookstore.

GAMES

- Read the first lines from a variety of favorite stories, and have the kids guess the book.
- Ask trivia questions about popular books, and have a two-team contest to guess the answers.
- Hand out picture books, juvenile books, or young adult books, one to each guest. Have the kids sit in a circle and read the first line or each book, one at a time, to form a funny new story.

ACTIVITIES

- Let the kids create their own storybooks. Supply the paper and writing

VARIATIONS

- Arrange a special story hour with your local children's librarian and take the kids to the library for an adventure with books.
- Help the kids get their own library cards if they haven't got one already.

HELPFUL HINT

- Teach the kids how to handle books carefully—especially library books—so they learn to appreciate them.

TIME MACHINE PARTY

It's fun to rediscover old stuff that you've long forgotten. This time capsule party will transport the kids from the present to the past—but it won't happen until the future!

INVITATIONS

- Write the party details on a scroll, burn the edges of the paper, roll it up, and tie it with a ribbon. Mail the scrolls in padded envelopes or hand-deliver to the kids.
- Borrow baby pictures of each guest, photocopy them several times at a copy store, and write the party details on the backs. Mail to guests.
- For added fun, make a collage of all the guests' baby pictures, and make copies to use as the invitations.

COSTUMES

- Have the kids come dressed as babies or toddlers.
- Ask the kids to bring something special from the past, such as blankets or

teddy bears. Provide pacifier necklaces and decorated juice bottles when the kids arrive.
- Have the kids come as they may look in the future.

TIME CAKE

1. Bake a round cake according to package directions; cool.
2. Frost the cake with white frosting.
3. Using frosting tubes, draw the face of a clock, with the numbers and the hands.
4. Use different color frosting for the number that reflects the child's age (if making this cake for a birthday).

DECORATIONS

- Display baby items throughout the party room. Include bottles, diapers, pacifiers, baby equipment, and so on. Borrow items from friends with babies if you don't have the items on hand.

- Check a poster store for funny baby pictures to hang on the walls, and display baby pictures of the guests.
- Secretly borrow some old toys from the kids, and feature them on the party table.
- Enlarge recent pictures of the kids, cut off the heads, and paste the heads onto new bodies. It's fun to select actors and performer, such as Arnold Schwarzenegger and Madonna.

GAMES
- Display the kids' baby pictures, and have them try to guess who's who.
- Find some baby pictures of Hollywood stars, and have the kids try to guess their identities.
- Put a bunch of baby items into paper bags, and have the kids feel inside the bags to guess the items.
- Show the kids magazine ads for baby products. Cut out the product names, and have the kids try to guess the products.

• Hold up each item you've borrowed from guests' homes, and ask the others players to guess to whom the toys belong.

ACTIVITY

• Put together a group time capsule. Have the kids decide what should go into the capsule. You might want to include a newspaper, a popular toy, a class picture, a comic book, an article of fad clothing, and so on. Seal the items in a small metal box, and bury it in the backyard. Tell the kids you will all meet in five or ten years, dig up the box, and see what's inside!

VARIATIONS

• Visit a history museum where the kids are likely to see objects from the past.
• Compare museum items to things from the present, and have the kids project what things might be like in the future.
• If possible, visit a futuristic museum.

HELPFUL HINT

• Be careful with original photographs. Copy stores can make color copies of precious photographs, so you can borrow the kids' pictures, have copies made, and return them immediately, with little risk of loss.

FOOD

• Feed the kids mashed up favorites, such as applesauce, puréed fruit, mashed potatoes, and other baby-like food. Serve everything in baby food jars.
• Let the kids drink from baby bottles, too!

FAVORS

• Give the kids baby bottles filled with jelly beans or other treats.
• Give each kid a diary to keep track of the upcoming year.
• Hand out scrapbooks so the kids can keep time capsules of their own over the years.

TOON TOWN PARTY

Move into Toon Town for a party full of animated fun. Have your child choose his or her favorite comic or cartoon character, and use it as your theme for everything—from invitations to favors. When the kids see Mickey, Minnie, Bugs, or Popeye at the party, they'll go Looney Tunes!

INVITATIONS

- Make one copy of a favorite cartoon character for each guest. Fold the sheets of paper into invitations, and make speech bubbles inviting the kids to the party.
- Create a cartoon character with the body of Mickey Mouse or Bugs Bunny and the head of an invited guest! Make photocopies of the character and of the guest photo, cut and paste onto a card, and you've got a personalized Toon Town invitation.

COSTUMES

- Have the kids come dressed as their favorite cartoon character. On the invitation, give the kids lots of characters from which to choose, including Mickey Mouse, Bugs Bunny, Road Runner, Beavis and Butthead, Bart Simpson, Porky Pig, Sylvester the Cat, Tweety Bird, Animaniacs, and so on.

DECORATIONS

- Tape cutouts of cartoon characters all around the room.
- Use comic books as place mats.

- Hang posters of your kid's favorite cartoon critters on the walls.
- Place small plastic figures of cartoon characters on the table to form a centerpiece.
- Run a Disney movie in the background, or play music from Disneyland.
- Use lots of balloons to fill the room with color, and draw cartoon faces on each of the balloons.

GAMES

- Play Name That Cartoon. Have the kids listen to cartoon jingles and guess the name of the shows.
- Cover up cartoon characters, and let the kids peek at just the eyes or mouths of characters and try to guess who they are.
- Have the kids act out cartoon characters while the others try to guess the characters.
- Cut pictures of cartoon characters into puzzle pieces. Have the kids race to assemble their puzzles.
- To make the puzzle game harder, put all the puzzle pieces into one big pile, and have the kids find the pieces that belong to their puzzle.

ACTIVITIES

- Let the kids create their own cartoon characters, complete with costumes and funny names. Have the kids use crepe paper and thrift-store accessories, such as jewelry, hats, gloves, vests, jackets, shoes, and wigs, to create the costumes.
- Have the kids make a giant cartoon panel. Have the kids draw cartoon characters on square sheets of white paper. Then have them fill in speech bubbles, saying something about the pictures. Line the pictures along the wall, and read the cartoon panel from start to finish. Enjoy the silly story.

CARTOON CHARACTER CAKE

1. Buy a cartoon cake mold at a party store, or make a cartoon shape yourself with some creative carving. Easy faces to make include Mickey Mouse, Miss Piggy, Daffy Duck, and Bart Simpson.
2. Frost the cake with white frosting.
3. Add details with frosting tubes.

FOOD

- Serve the cartoon characters' favorite foods, such as carrots for Bugs Bunny, succotash for Sylvester, and spinach for Popeye.

• Supply the kids with cut-up veggies and fruits and a variety of spreads, and let them make open-face cartoon sandwiches on white bread.

FAVORS

• Send the kids home with little plastic figurines of cartoon characters.
• Give the kids favorite comic books.
• Offer the kids inexpensive cartoon videos they can watch at home.
• Give the kids cassettes featuring music from the latest popular animated movie.

VARIATIONS

• Take the kids to a screening of a new Disney or other animated movie.
• Buy the kids popcorn at the movie, or take along baggies of popcorn and a small box of candy from home.
• Instead of a Cartoon Character Cake, make a Toon Town Cake. Bake a round cake, frost it with green-tinted frosting, cover it with green coconut for grass, and set small plastic cartoon figures on top.

HELPFUL HINT

• Watch a popular cartoon video to get ideas for your party.

TRASH BASH PARTY

Recycle the fun over and over again, with a Trash Bash celebration. Help save the planet as you party, and come away with lots of homemade toys and games, all created from throwaways. The best part is—a Trash Bash doesn't cost a lot to host!

INVITATIONS

- Use old newspapers to create your trash bash invitations. Hand print or use your computer to create an article with the party details. Make copies, and cut-and-paste them into real newspaper pages. When the kids read the headlines, they'll find they're invited to a party!
- Send the invitations in envelopes made from recycled paper, of course.

COSTUMES

- Ask the kids to dress creatively, using old junk in a new way. With a little recy-

RECYCLED CUPCAKES

1. Prepare cupcake batter.
2. Clean a variety of small cans, such as tuna, olive, and tomato sauce. Remove all jagged edges.
3. Spray the cans with vegetable spray.
4. Pour cupcake batter into the cans.
5. Bake according to package directions; cool.
6. Frost the cupcakes with chocolate and white frosting, and top with sprinkles leftover from former parties.
7. Serve the cupcakes in the cans.

cled paper, cut-up plastic, or clean cans, the guests can use their imaginations to create a whole new/old look!

DECORATIONS

- Cover the party table with old newspapers.
- Serve drinks in a variety of clean plastic bottles, cans with smooth edges, and other recyclables.

GAMES

- Make a Jai Alai game from clean, plastic, gallon-sized milk cartons. Cut off the tops, leaving the handles intact, and give one to each guest. Have the kids toss a tennis ball back and forth between the Jai Alai scoops.
- Make tennis rackets from old wire hangars and nylons. Pull the hanger into diamond shapes, cover with old nylons, tie them off, and use the "rackets" to hit tennis balls back and forth. (If you do this inside, make sure to remove all breakables from the party room.)

ACTIVITIES

- Make Squirt Birds from old plastic squirt bottles. Clean the bottles thoroughly, then let the kids draw funny faces on the tops of the bottles—birds, monsters, or whatever they like. Add beaks or other details with pom-poms or plastic margarine-tub cutouts. Secure with a glue gun. Take the Squirt Birds outside and have a water war.
- Make candle holders. Clean small cans, such as tuna or olive cans, and paint the cans with acrylic paint, or cover them with colorful Contact paper. Fill with pieces of old or broken candles, fill in the spaces with paraffin wax, add new wicks, and you have new recycled candles!
- Make sock puppets. Give the kids permanent felt-tip pens, and have them draw eyes, noses, and mouths on old

- Serve food on cleaned foil or plastic TV dinner trays.
- Get mismatched silverware from friends or a thrift store.
- Make a centerpiece out of old clean socks turned into puppets. Make one for each guest to take home at the end of the party.
- Place "recycle" stickers around the room and on the guests as they arrive.

socks. Slip the sock onto your hand, and watch the puppet come to life.

- Award prizes for costumes. Make sure every guest gets a prize by having lots of different categories, such as most interesting, best use of plastic, most likely to go straight to the dump, and so on.

FOOD

- Serve old favorites and call them "leftovers," even if they aren't!
- Combine macaroni and cheese with a box of frozen vegetables to make it look like yesterday's dinner.
- Make spaghetti noodles and serve them with a variety of choose-it-yourself toppings.
- Give the kids burritos filled with beans, meat, and veggies, and call them Kitchen Sink Burritos.

VARIATIONS

- Attend an Earth Day or Recycle event with the kids, so they can see recycling in action.
- Take the kids to a recycling plant where newspapers, bottles, or cans are made into new and useful products.

HELPFUL HINT

- Make sure recycled bottles, cans, and other containers are thoroughly cleaned and all the edges are smoothed before using them.

FAVORS

- Give the kids recycled stationery.
- Send the kids home with the sock puppets.
- Give the kids fancy new wastebaskets covered with Contact paper or painted with flowers. Tell them to use them to recycle at home.
- Offer scarves made from old dresses purchased from a thrift store.
- Hand out "collector boxes" made from recycled margarine tubs or other containers.

UPSIDE-DOWN, INSIDE-OUT, AND BACKWARDS PARTY

The kids will feel like Alice in Wonderland when they attend this upside-down, inside-out, and backwards party. Remember to do the opposite of what you usually do and you can't go wrong—er...right! Now, "don't" invite the guests and "don't" have a good time! (Opposite!)

INVITATIONS

- Write the party details on the backs of the invitations, and write the information upside down and backwards so your guests have to decipher it. Fold the cards inside out, and place them in the envelopes upside down. Address the backs of the envelopes, instead of the fronts. (Make sure you write the addresses correctly or they may not get there!)

COSTUMES

- Ask the kids to dress in clothes they have put on inside out, upside down, and backwards. They may arrive with their pants turned inside out, their shirts put on backwards, and their socks worn over their shoes! Anything goes, as long as everything is put on slightly off!

DECORATIONS

- Greet your guests facing backwards, and tell them "not" to come in.
- Hang posters upside down.

- Hang balloons by string from the ceiling so they appear upside down.
- Turn knickknacks in the party room upside down.
- Set up the party food under the table, and have the kids sit on the floor—under the table—to enjoy the party treats.
- Set the cups and plates upside down and the silverware backwards.
- Play a video in the background, but run it on slow rewind.

GAMES

- Play your favorite games—but with a twist: backwards!
- Instead of pinning the tail on the donkey's rear, pin it on the nose!
- Play musical chairs, but instead of finding a seat when the music stops playing, find one when it begins!
- Have a bunch of relay races in the backyard, and run them all backwards!
- Play a board game backwards!
- Have the kids dress normally, and choose one player to leave the room.

UPSIDE-DOWN CAKE

1. Bake a packaged pineapple upside-down cake, or use a favorite recipe.
2. Turn the cake out of the baking pan in front of the kids so they can see the surprise topping when you flip it upside down.
3. Use colored alphabet macaroni noodles to write the kids' names backwards on the cake.
4. Make upside-down ice-cream sundaes to go with the cake: Begin with the toppings, and pile on the sundae ingredients until you end up with ice cream on top. Or make inverted ice-cream cones: Scoop balls of ice cream onto small plates, top with ice-cream cones, and let the kids decorate the cones with frosting tubes to make clowns, monsters, or anything they like.

While the player is gone, have one guest turn an article of clothing inside out, backwards, or upside down. When the player returns, have him or her guess which guest made a change and what it was.

ACTIVITIES

- Try drawing backwards. Give guests sheets of paper and set them in front of a mirror. Place a picture facing the mirror, and have the kids copy the picture without looking at it. They may look only in the mirror as a guide. See who can make the best drawing—it won't be easy!
- Tell a round-robin story, but begin at the end, and have the kids continue the story—backwards!

• Make Tornadoes in a Bottle. Clean large plastic drink bottles and fill them three-quarters full with colored water. Fill the rest of the bottle with oil and glitter. Seal the lid with glue. Have the kids swirl the bottles and turn them upside down to see the tornado.

FOOD

• Make inside-out sandwiches. Place the filling on top of the bread slices, instead of inside.
• Make an upside-down fruit salad. Place a cherry at the bottom of a bowl, sprinkle some chopped nuts on top, add a spoonful of vanilla yogurt or whipped cream, then add the fruit. Cover with a lettuce leaf, and serve. Let the kids eat it as is, or turn the salad out onto a plate for a surprise.

• Serve soup with a fork, peas with a small plastic knife, and spaghetti with a spoon.

FAVORS

• Give the kids mirrors so they can do backwards things at home.
• Offer the kids comic books, with the covers stapled on upside down.
• Let the kids take home the Tornadoes in the Bottles they made.
• Give the kids snowstorm jars that must be turned upside down to see the snow fall. You can buy these or make them yourself. (See Snow Sculpture Party.)
• Offer the kids anything that can be turned upside down, inside out, or backwards.

VARIATION

• Instead of an Upside-Down, Inside-Out, and Backwards Party, host a Big/Little Party, in which everything is either very big or very little.

HELPFUL HINT

• Give "tickets" to the kids every time they make a violation and don't do something upside down, inside out, or backwards. The player with the fewest tickets wins an upside-down prize!

WAKE-UP PARTY

This is a surprise party, but not for the guest of honor. It's a surprise for the invited guests! And even better—it happens at the crack of dawn, so the kids come as they are! This party is truly a wake-up call that will get the kids "up 'n' at 'em!"

INVITATIONS

- You won't need invitations, since the guests don't know they are invited to a party! But you do have to let the parents know ahead of time. Call the parents when you think the invited guests aren't around, and explain the party details. Tell them what day and time you're coming to wake up the kids—and that they are NOT to tell them. Ask the parents to have robes and slippers ready.
- If you prefer, send an invitation to the guests to let them know a party is being planned, but tell them the date and time are a surprise!

COSTUMES

- Pajamas, of course. Tell the kids to come to the party in their sleeping clothes, robes, and slippers.

SUNSHINE CAKE

1. Set a cluster of cinnamon rolls together to form a large circle.
2. Frost the rolls with yellow-tinted cream cheese frosting.
3. Make a face on the sun using cut-up fruit.

- If the kids' pajamas aren't appropriate to be worn outside the house, let the kids put on another layer, but don't let them change!
- Have the guest of honor also wear pajamas while collecting all the guests.

DECORATIONS

- Decorate the dining room or kitchen to look like an early-morning diner.
- Cut out a big yellow sun to greet the guests at the front door.
- Make "Good Morning" posters. Write "Good Morning" in several different languages on sheets of paper, and hang the posters on the walls.
- Drape the ceiling in yellow and orange crepe paper, and dangle personalized toothbrushes from the center.
- Place bright yellow balloons around the party room to help wake up the kids.

GAMES

- Bring along a tape recorder as you wake the kids, and tape the scene. Play back the tape at the party and see if everyone can guess who's being awakened.
- Have a pillow fight!

FOOD

- Offer a cereal buffet. Place lots of choices on the table, and let the kids put together whatever they want.
- Serve choose-it-yourself omelets. Add the kids' favorite ingredients that they select from bowls on the counter.
- Serve decaffeinated mochas in coffee cups to wash it all down.

FAVORS

- Give the kids personalized toothbrushes to take home.
- Let the kids take home the makeup and hair products they used.
- Hand out coffee mugs when the mochas are all gone.

- Set out a number of morning items, such as a toothbrush, a newspaper, a coffee cup, and a cereal box, and have the kids study the items for one minute. Remove the items and see how many items the kids can recall.
- Go around the circle and have each player name one item. Let that player keep the item he or she named.

ACTIVITIES

- Model nightware for one another, and put on a pajama fashion show, complete with a narrator who can point out the fashion statements in detail.
- Do one another's makeup and hair, using lots of inexpensive lipsticks, blushes, powders, nail polish, brushes, combs, and mousse.
- Have a pajama parade down the street!

VARIATION

- Have the party at an early morning diner, instead of at home! Warn the restaurant you'll be coming, so they can set up the tables. Tell them the kids will be dressed in their pajamas, so they won't be too shocked. Then enjoy breakfast while the other breakfast-eaters enjoy your company.

HELPFUL HINTS

- Tell the parents to warn their kids to wear decent pajamas. Ask them to try not to give it away, though!
- Provide separate makeup for each kid and discourage sharing to avoid infection.

WILD WEST PARTY

Make the Wild West your theme, and host a rodeo party for the young cowpokes. You can play lots of outdoor games to simulate the Old West and to bring back the fun of the new frontier. So saddle up, young'un, it's time to ride into the sunset.

INVITATIONS
- Send the cowboy and cowgirl guests official "sheriff" badges. You can buy them at party stores or make them from cardboard cut into stars and covered with foil.
- Write the party details on a "Wanted" poster, using your special guest of honor as the "villain." Attach the sheriff's badge to the poster. Mail in large envelopes.

COSTUMES
- Ask the kids to come dressed as cowpokes, horseback riders, sheriffs, dance-hall gals, or anything related to the Wild West.
- Add bandannas, badges, and belt buckles as accessories.

SHERIFF'S STAR CAKE
1. Bake two square cakes; cool.
2. Cut one cake into five triangles.
3. Place the triangles on the sides of the whole cake.
4. Frost the cake, and decorate it with the names of heroes from the old West.

DECORATIONS
- Decorate your backyard to look like a rodeo or ranch.
- Put up "Wanted" outlaw posters on the fence.
- Hang up lassos and cowboy hats around the party room.
- Create store signs for typical Old-West merchants stores, such as blacksmith, livery, and dry goods.
- Rope off a "corral" for the games.
- Set up a stagecoach made from a large cardboard box and an old sheet.
- If you have any sawhorses, turn them into dummy horses for fun.

GAMES
- Have a lasso contest to see what the kids can round up. Tie a rope into a large circle, and have the kids take turns trying to toss it around a sawhorse or other inanimate object.
- Play a one-legged game of tag. Have everyone hop to safety to the other side of the "corral".
- Play a game of horseshoes.

FOOD

- At the campfire, roast hot dogs, marsh-mallows, and eat pork and beans from a tin plate.
- Make pigs in a blanket by wrapping bis-cuit dough around cocktail wieners and heating them in the oven.

FAVORS

- Send the rustlers home with plastic cow-boys.
- Give the kids bandannas and belt buck-les to wear home.
- Give the kids water guns to cool off.
- Offer inexpensive Western videos.

VARIATIONS

- Host the party at a real ranch, and take the kids horseback riding for the main event.
- Rent a Western video and watch it while eating hot dogs and beans.
- Instead of a Sheriff's Star Cake, make the following cake: Bake a sheet cake, frost with green-tinted frosting, cover with green-tinted coconut to make grass, and decorate with plastic cowboys, horses, and "corral" fences.

HELPFUL HINT

- This is an outdoor party, so have alternative plans in case of rain.

ACTIVITIES

- Set up a gambling casino in the "saloon" and play cards, roulette, checkers, coin toss, and other games.
- Do some squirt-gun sharpshooting. Set up lightweight plastic bottles on a fence or table, and have the kids shoot them off for points.
- Tell Wild West stories around a camp-fire.

INDEX

G

Kids' Party Games and Activities

by Penny Warner
Illustrated by Kathy Rogers

This is the most complete guide to party games and activities for kids ages 2–12! It contains illustrated descriptions, instructions, rules, and trouble-shooting tips for 300 games and activities (more than triple the number in other books), including traditional and contemporary games, and simple and elaborate activities, plus ideas for outings, events, and entertainers.

Order #6095 $12.00

Kids' Holiday Fun

by Penny Warner
Illustrated by Kathy Rogers

Penny Warner's new book gives you fun ideas for entertaining your children at 34 different holidays, including New Year's, Valentine's Day, St. Patrick's Day, Fourth of July, Halloween, and Christmas. Every month of the year, your family can turn to this comprehensive guide for holiday recipes, decoration suggestions, instructions for fun holiday activities and games, party ideas, and crafts.

Order #6000 $12.00

Kids' Party Cookbook

by Penny Warner
Illustrated by Laurel Aiello

Over 175 reduced-fat recipes with food that's fun and tasty for kids but full of nutrition to please parents. Warner has fun ideas for every meal, including mini-meals, such as Peanut Butter Burger Dogs and Twinkle Sandwiches; creative snacks, such as Aquarium Jello and Prehistoric Bugs; nutritious drinks, such as Beetle Juice and Apple Jazz; creative desserts, such as Spaghetti Ice Cream; and holiday fare, such as Jack O' Lantern Custard for Halloween. (Ages 8 and up)

Order #2435 $12.00

Kids Are Cookin'

by Karen Brown
Illustrated by Laurel Aiello

Here are 100 all-time-favorite, kid-pleasing recipes for everything from snacks and drinks to entrées and desserts. These are the recipes that kids like best, passed on from one generation to the next, written in a style that makes cooking fun for kids.

Order #2440 $8.00

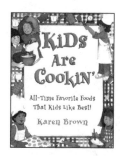

Order Form

Qty.	Title	Author	Order No.	Unit Cost (U.S. $)	Total
	Bad Case of the Giggles	Lansky, B.	2411	$15.00	
	Best Birthday Party Game Book	Lansky, B.	6064	$3.95	
	Best Party Book	Warner, P.	6089	$8.00	
	Free Stuff for Kids	Free Stuff Editors	2190	$5.00	
	Girls to the Rescue	Lansky, B.	2215	$3.95	
	Girls to the Rescue, Book #2	Lansky, B.	2216	$3.95	
	Girls to the Rescue, Book #3	Lansky, B.	2219	$3.95	
	Happy Birthday to Me	Lansky, B.	2416	$9.95	
	Kids Are Cookin'	Brown, P.	2440	$8.00	
	Kids' Holiday Fun	Warner, P.	6000	$12.00	
	Kids' Party Cookbook	Warner, P.	2435	$12.00	
	Kids' Party Games and Activities	Warner, P.	6095	$12.00	
	Kids' Pick-A-Party Book	Warner, P.	6090	$9.00	
	Kids Pick the Funniest Poems	Lansky, B.	2410	$15.00	
	New Adventures of Mother Goose	Lansky, B.	2420	$15.00	
	Newfangled Fairy Tales	Lansky, B.	2500	$3.95	
	No More Homework! No More Tests!	Lansky, B.	2414	$8.00	
	Poetry Party	Lansky, B.	2430	$15.00	
	Young Marian's Adventures	Mooser, S.	2218	$4.50	
				Subtotal	
		Shipping and Handling (see below)			
		MN residents add 6.5% sales tax			
				Total	

YES! Please send me the books indicated above. Add $2.00 shipping and handling for the first book and 50¢ for each additional book. Add $2.50 to total for books shipped to Canada. Overseas postage will be billed. Allow up to four weeks for delivery. Send check or money order payable to Meadowbrook Press. No cash or C.O.D's please. Prices subject to change without notice. **Quantity discounts available upon request.**

Send book(s) to:

Name _____ Address _____

City _____ State _____ Zip _____

Telephone (_____)_____ P.O. number (if necessary) _____

Payment via:

❑ Check or money order payable to Meadowbrook Press (No cash or C.O.D.'s please)

Amount enclosed $ _____

❑ Visa (for orders over $10.00 only) ❑ MasterCard (for orders over $10.00 only)

Account # _____ Signature _____ Exp. Date _____

A *FREE* Meadowbrook Press catalog is available upon request.
You can also phone us for orders of $10.00 or more at 1-800-338-2232.

Mail to: Meadowbrook Press
5451 Smetana Drive, Minnetonka, MN 55343
Toll-Free 1-800-338-2232

Phone (612) 930-1100

Fax (612) 930-1940